Wonderful World of

WRITING, ACTING & PUBLISHING PROJECT FOR YOUNGSTERS

10 Years of Inspirational Writing and Art
By Over 100 Young Contributors

Edited by
Grace Quansah

PUBLISHED BY KRIK KRAK

First published in 2018 in Great Britain
Krik Krak
Unit H, Dean Way
Great Western Industrial Park
London UB2 4SB

Krik Krak is an imprint of Cross Culture Media

Copyright of the individual poems and stories
remains with the individual authors
© Contributors 2018

Edited by Grace Quansah

ISBN 978-1-908415-06-6

Publishing project supported with the kind help of
Arts Council England

Book and cover design by Mervyn Weir

Printed in UK

*"One child, one teacher,
one book and one pen
can change the world"*

Malala Yousafza
Pakistani Child Activist and Nobel Peace Prize Winner, 2013

Contents

Acknowledgements

This book has come about because of the support, inspirations and collaborations of many generous, individuals and bodies, all friends of WAPPY, over the past ten years. I wish to express a simple thanks to as many supporters as I can:

Arts Council England (ACE), Ifilia Francois/Positive Awareness Charity, Eric Huntley and the late Jessica Huntley/Bogle L'Ouverture Press, Judy Wellington/Lifeline Learning Centre, Maureen Roberts/London Metropolitan Archives, Tranzition Agency, Sally Baffour and Esther Ackah;

The trustees of WAPPY, John Durston (advisor), Carolyn Warner, Anjan Saha, Manjinder Chijarh, Regina Ioannou, Marie Ikong-Ehuy and former trustees, Dr. Graham Shaw, Debbie Hughes, and Marcia K Ellis;

Past and current volunteers, Ursula Troche, Robert Williams, Ray Johnson, Benson Chinenzura, Deepa Patel, Deka Ibrahim, Patricia Adams, Nicola O'Brien, Rahwa Ghergish, Anna Khanzadi, Rashmi Das, Michelle Evans, Lily Kalnakova, Jane Harris, Lorenz McCloud, Lorraine Ryan, Christine Francis, Melanie Hughes, Tony Rowe, Esther Ramnath, Lindsay Warner and Gloria Bustamante;

Major sponsors and collaborators including Ealing's Youth & Connexions/ Summer University/Sarah Constable, Ealing Grants Unit/Delores Graham, Matt Freidson, Reos Partners, Big Lottery (Awards for All), Help a Capital Child, Near Neighbours (Church Fund)/David Marsden and Elizabeth Fewkes, Kyria Consulting Limited/Dave Conlon and Ruth Conlon, Random House Children's Books/Sue Cook,Shangwe/ Nicole Moore, Tamarind Books/Verna Wilkins, Cultural Community Solutions (Ealing)/ Ealing Libraries, Acton Community Forum/Steve Flynn/ ARTification/ Rachel Pepper, Bollo United/Huey Reid, Circular Training Group/Cheryl Burke, Groove Control DJS/Pascoe Sawyers, Ealing Volunteer Services/Wendy Sender, Black History, Culture & West London, Pozi-Planet, ALKM/Nostalgia Steel Band,/Dr. Lionel McCalman, Black Londoners Appeal/ Caroline

Obonyo, Mike Kavanagh (The Scrumbler), Anansesem/Summer Edward (Caribbean), Laura Thomas/Laura Thomas Communications (Canada), Leanne Creatives, Insights School and Skills Academy/Barbara Quartey MBE, Brunel University (Pro-Active West), Gess Productions, Lyric Theatre/Charlotte Davies, Beck Theatre/Catherine Goss, JaeGenious, Smile Be Happy Photography/Lalita Scott, West Twyford Youth & Community Project/Anthony Smith, Hot Key Books/Rosi Crawley, IBA Colourview/Guy Hamilton, Knight, Sound & Light, Easy Tees, Essequibo Music/Keith Waithe, West Twyford Primary School/Rachel Martin, Christ the Saviour CofE Primary School, KSD Martial Arts/Christine Francis, On The Ball FC/CJ Ramson, Walpole Park/Alys Hughes, Grenadian Sunshine Foundation/Yvonne Gabriel, Youth Street Beats/ Collette Noel, Descendants/ Margaret Noel, Old Oak Primary School/ Vicki Joshua, Twyford CofE High School, Brentside High School, Duane Jay, St Mary's Church (West Twyford)/ Simon Reed, St Dunstan's Church/Jon Westall, KA Filmworks/ Khesumaba Jess, DM Folk Collective/ Tamsin Durston, Phil McMullan, David Berkovitch, London Network Church/Alex Afriyie/David and Nadine Peart/Claire Gibbons/ Morrisons (W3), Tesco's (W5) Nando's (W5), Waterstones (W5), Lidl (W7), Marks & Spencer (W5), Salam Supermarket (East Acton), Acton Hill Gospel Chorale, Runaway Entertainment/ Laura Elmes, Hypnotick Dance/ Taofeeq 'Taz' Sanusi, Transcultural Visions/Bilkis Malik, Recognition Express/Andy Lian, Ealing Gazette, Voice Newspaper, Ealing Apprenticeships/Vanita Nicholls, University of West London/ Hospitality;

Nii Ayikwei Parkes, Vivian French, Will Mellor, James Barnor, Henry Bonsu, Olusola Oyeleye, Jan Blake, Sandra Agard, Mia Morris, Sharon Walters, Sheila Gumbi, Jack Shalloo, Ruby Tandoh, JC Lodge, Errol O'Meally, Gia Re, Danita McIntyre, Aamasade Shepnekhi, Siayoum Karuma, Kwabena Amen, Rasheda Ashanti, Doreen Joseph, Marcia Gordon, Adra Nelson, Claire Cooke, Yetunde Reuben, Amina Blackwood Meeks, Chinyere Nwaubani, Chinwe Ojielo, Asha, Christina Tom-Johnson, Councillor Shahbaz, Berenice Miles, Nick Hunt, Joshua Hunt, Vijay Amin, Linda Davies, Gillian Spragg, Amma Poku, Karen Henry, Martha Lambert, Lee Stallard, Fiona Tarn, Tracy Tunstall, Kiran Sharma, Rabin Bose, Justinder

Kudhail, Grant Bavister, Colin Prescod, Mike McKenzie, Georgiana Jackson-Callen, Jai Ellis, Cassius Jackson-Callen, Jojo Yates, Lascelles James, Steve Cole, Marlo Webster, Dorothea Smartt, Pasty Isles, Jackie Sear, Michelle Yaa Asantewa, TUUP, June Tuitt, Tim Beckerley, Yvonne Field, Wendy Sharpe, Dr. Reverend Jennifer Smith, Serina and Harry Goulborne, Keith Clowe, Richard O'Conor, Lillia Nelson, Steven Hutchinson, Brian Altchuler, Dr. Charles Armah, Jnr., Hilary Nicholl Bartle, James Cameron Cooper, Jessica Burbury, Sanghita Shah, Elfat Darwich, Becca Sokal and Sangeeta Bajaj, Deborah Klayman, Cherry & Ian Vaughan, Michelle Dawkins, Fiona Barakat, Toyin Agbetu, Charlie Payne;

All WAPPY parents and family helpers including Benjamin Pozi-Quansah, Anthony Pozi Quansah, Jasmine Walcott, Hagar Eshun, Colin Grant, Ulrich Quee, Faith Miller, Joan Jackson-Callen, MBE, Nana Yaa Forsuah, Marie Mostaeddi, Nina Bindra, Angela Plumber, Janet Plummer, Aurora Sebastiano, Khawla Allawi, Azhar Abed, Alma James, Karen Thomas, Ibi Showunmi and Sian Sim;

Professor Benjamin Zephaniah, Patrice Lawrence, Dr. Rupa Huq MP. (Central Ealing & Acton), Councillor Julian Bell, Carole Stewart, Sebastian Jenner, Marge Lowhar, Mervyn Weir and Alydia R. Thompson.

Finally, I wish to express an enormous thank you to each young person who has contributed to WAPPY since its beginning in 2008, whether writer, spoken word artist and/or musician, because of getting involved in a single workshop or a combination of workshops or successive projects, which have led to the production of this landmark anthology. Thank you for writing imaginatively and bravely. Thank you for simply writing. Thank you for your artwork. Most of all Thank you for being you!

Grace Quansah *(Akuba)*

foreword

The first writing I ever had published was a poem. I had sent it to the Brighton Evening Argus when I was thirteen and was thrilled when I received an acceptance letter. I still have it. Not only was I paid - the queenly sum of £1 via postal order - but I knew that everybody who bought that newspaper in that pre-internet age would see my poem.

For me, poetry was an essential part of my development as a writer. As a child, I recorded family events in poetry. So when the coffee percolator exploded, coating ceiling, wall and dog in grounds, did I help clear up? No, I wrote a poem about it. When my mum came screaming out of an Italian forest with a worm the size of a snake wrapped round her ankle, did I comfort her? No, I wrote a poem about it. I even submitted my Year 7 history homework in rhyme. Twice. And the lovely teacher gave me an A both times.

As an adult, I have come to understand the enduring impact of poetry. One of my mum's friends, a widow of many years, recently asked me if I still have the poem I wrote about her husband more than forty years ago. The first family who looked after me, while my single mother was training to be a nurse, say they still have the poems I wrote for them when I was seven. My mum quotes Tennyson ('The Book' has been a part of my life for as long as I can remember) and Robert Louis Stevenson's 'In the Land of Counterpane'. My novel for teenagers, 'Indigo Donut', starts with Grace Nichols' 'Praise Song for My Mother', as it so beautifully embodies the book's themes of what we want a mother to be.

The works in this fantastic WAPPY anthology show us that poetry is so apt at capturing a mood, a moment, a person. They can build narratives out of words, turn unexpected corners and hum with joy or sadness. As the school curriculum offers fewer opportunities for self-expression and exploration of the arts just for the joy of it, organisations such as WAPPY are vital. I know that without poetry and encouragement as a child, I would not be writing award-winning books now.

In the pages that follow, you will read from the future poets and authors and illustrators who, thanks to WAPPY, believe that their voices matter. Right now, that feels essential.

Patrice Lawrence
Author of Granny Ting Ting
Orangeboy - Winner of The Bookseller's YA Book Prize 2017,
the Waterstones Children's Book Prize for Older Children 2017,
and shortlisted for the 2016 Costa Children's Book Award.
Indigo Donut - Shortlisted for the Bookseller YA Prize
Snap - World Book Day 2019

An Overview by Eric Huntley

HAPPY BIRTHDAY W.A.P.P.Y.

The genesis of WAPPY ('Writing, Acting & Publishing Project for Youngsters') could partly be traced to the birth of the Acton Black History Group in 2003. The Group became aware of the need to record and celebrate the contributions of the Black communities in Acton.

It was this 'Grounding' which was the spark that provided WAPPY with a firm publishing base, as well as collaborating with the older generation and empowering the young, from multi-ethnic backgrounds, however, with a large African-descended and Asian-descended contingent.

Initially, based in Hanwell at the Lifeline Learning Academy, the work-shops attracted young people, not just from within the Ealing borough but from several neighbouring boroughs including Brent, Hillingdon and Hounslow. As time progressed WAPPY offered holiday and term-time workshops at different locations, (i.e. Acton, Ealing, Hanwell, and Southall), while expanding its provision across London and beyond.

The decade has not been without its challenges, however under the guidance of its indefatigable coordinator, Grace, the organisation has been able to obtain the support of a wide range of bodies, including, The London Metropolitan Archives, Tamarind Books, Random House Children's Books, Shangwe and Bogle L'Ouverture Publications and others.

One of the greatest pleasures over the years has been to witness the growth in confidence and ability of students from a wide cross section of the community while 'showcasing' their skills in the field of Writing and Acting and eventually becoming published authors in their own right.

I am sure that it was this atmosphere of creativity generated by the young that provided the energy and spirit for Esther Ackah to complete her publication of 'Mame Nwia-Amah: Ghana's Undiscovered Divine Healer, Prophetess and Carer' in 2015. A packed audience at Ealing Central Library watched sisters, Maisa and Sara Abed, interview the new author about her book.

In my humble opinion Ms Ackah should be made an honourable member of WAPPY.

Eric Huntley
Patron, Bogle L'Ouverture Publications

10 Year Landmark Publication

I first came across WAPPY at the Annual Huntley Archives Conference at the LMA in 2009, a year after its birth. Amongst all the adult performances that year, was WAPPY's, and their presentation was a combination of song and performance poetry by various young people. Some of them were so young and confident in their performances, they stole everybody's heart. Their performances were so beautiful that it made a lasting impression on me.

A year later, in 2010, we invited teenage WAPPY members to participate in Thank U Charity's Youth Relief programme. In the aftermath of the 2010 Haiti earthquake, that caused unprecedented human disaster, young people from West London, including teenagers from WAPPY gathered for the Youth Relief Talent Competition/fundraiser in dance, music, spoken word/poetry and drama. To everyone's surprise and joy, the poetry prize was won by Georgiana Jackson-Callen, a 13-year-old member of WAPPY. Her confide-nt performance and recital of a poem she'd written for the competition, greatly impressed the young audience and all the judges; amongst whom was the renowned celebrated actor, Rudolph Walker OBE (who acts as Patrick Truman in the EastEnders TV Soap Opera).

My interest in WAPPY grew even more after that, inspiring me to attend several WAPPY's events. They seemed to get better every year, as one saw the young people developing and growing more confident in their performances, under the leadership of their very able and talented founder, Grace Quansah (aka 'Akuba').

Three years later, in 2013, I was invited by Jessica Huntley and Grace to be one of their Patrons. I felt honoured to be asked and gladly accepted it. Since then, I have watched the new members of WAPPY overcome their initial stage fright very quickly, as they grow into their talent and perform with confidence. Even more remarkable are the former members of WAPPY, who are thriving after moving on to higher institutions of study, to further their careers. Having gone on to University and excelled in their chosen careers, many are now doing very well as responsible members of society. This is an incredible achievement and testimony to the enduring positive influence that WAPPY now has on the children who have the good fortune of attending its programmes.

WAPPY has been a real gift to young people, especially in this digital age, when so many distractions are leading them astray. It has been a privilege for me to be linked with an organisation like WAPPY, that helps to develop and shape young minds, to become the self-confident, responsible, upright and the talented members of society, that we now see in those who have graduated from WAPPY's programmes since its inception, 10 years ago.

I'll also take this opportunity to congratulate WAPPY on their recent success in the Arts Council bid to fund the landmark publication, 'Wonderful World of WAPPY: 10 Years of Inspirational Writing and Art by Over 100 Young Writers'.

Long Live WAPPY!

Sally Baffour
Patron of WAPPY, Founder & CEO of Thank U Charity

WAPPY Has Become a Word

Something happens to me when I see or hear the word WAPPY, (because it has now become a word), something that's difficult to describe, and when I come into contact with the group those feelings just become more intense. A warm feeling goes through me because they bring me joy. Then I feel like I want to hug them all. The youngsters, the staff, the supporters (past and present), and everyone that has anything to do with the project is doing something close to my heart, so I want to keep them close to my heart. Then I feel the power. Not political power, or any power over others. I feel empowerment. I feel I'm surrounded by people who understand that the words they speak and write can empower them. They express themselves, they are heard, and they are standing up and being counted. Most of all I feel pride.

The term 'grass roots' can be so overused that after a time it can become meaningless. When used inappropriately by those who want to boost their own status it sounds like a sound bite. Not here. When you check the history of WAPPY and see how they have progressed over the years, the things they have done and the people they reach, you can be in no doubt that this is a real grass roots collective, with a real sense of purpose, that does what it says it does. It would be easy to say that they take young people and give them something to do, keeping them off the streets etc., but it's not as simple as that. These young people are encouraged to speak their minds creatively, and they always have something on the go, in other words, they are always doing it. This is what fills me with pride. They are filled with positivity, every project is enlightening, so every time I see or hear the word WAPPY, (because it has now become a word), I tell myself there is hope, and in turn I become filled with hope.

I'm not one for happy birthdays, happy Christmas, happy Easter etc., I just try to be happy every day, and appreciate every day, but there is something very special about WAPPY reaching ten years old. So I want to use this space to wish WAPPY a happy and glorious anniversary and wish you all the best for the future. Keep speaking your truths, keep telling your stories, keep singing your songs, and keep inspiring future generations, so for generations to come, (with reference to our ancestors), we can truly call ourselves the WAPPY family. Now that's what I call cool, this is what I call WAPPY, (because it has now become a word), and this is what I call an anniversary.

Benjamin Zephaniah
Poet, Playwright, Author, Musician & Professor of Creative Writing
at Brunel University, London

Why WAPPY? - It Has a Long Tale

WAPPY stands for Writing, Acting & Publishing Project for Youngsters. I came up with it in the kitchen of my London home whilst talking with my eldest son, Benjamin, one day in April 2008, but the idea behind WAPPY started many years before. To be honest, to understand how WAPPY came about we need to go back in time much further than ten years ago. We need to go back to the 1960s, long before any of the young people who have taken part in WAPPY today, were born. Long before even some of our WAPPY mums and dads were born.

In the 1960s when I was a little girl, I grew up for some of the time in Essex, a county in the south-east of England, north-east of London. From a baby of three months to a young girl of five years old, I lived with English 'Nanny and Daddy Clowe' and their son, Keith, who was my foster brother.

Not long after starting at the local school with Keith at five years old, my real parents (my biological mother and father) came for me. I spent a short time getting to know them while we travelled to Ghana, my country of origin in West Africa, on board a ship, which my father steered. I spent a couple of years in Ghana, with 'Uncle Vitus', my father's friend and his family. There, I went to a Catholic boarding school known as Ola, in Elmina (in Cape Coast), before returning to London to live with my real parents for good in the borough of Ealing. Back in London I settled down with my mother in Hanwell and went to Hobbayne Primary School from 1968 to 1973.

Being a child then was very confusing for me because I did not know if I belonged in Essex, Ghana or Hanwell. It was hard to figure out who my real parents were, and whether I saw myself as English, from Essex, or as Ghanaian, from Africa, or as 'Black' or 'white'. As strange as this may sound but in Ghana, no one saw me as a typical Ghanaian girl or as a typical 'Black' girl. Instead, the local people around me, especially in the rural areas of Accra (its capital), Cape Coast and further, referred to me in their 'mother tongue' as the 'white English girl'. This 'clash' of identity and having to ask questions about belonging are themes which our contributors explore in the chapter 'Where do I belong'.

I was scared to make friends because I feared that I would soon have to pack my bags again and leave home, leave school and leave good friends behind. I had to get used to change more than most children of my age could be expected to do from around four to seven years old. And that upheaval continued well into my teenage years. By age thirteen, thanks to changes in the education system brought about by the Labour government in power during the mid-1970s, I found myself having to move to two different secondary schools within two years. Then when I was fourteen years old, on 19th February 1976 my real father passed away quite suddenly in Ghana. He worked for the Black Star Line Shipping Company, which was based there, and was due to return to England but he never made it. I never got the chance to say good bye to him.

So being a child was very hard to deal with, but I had one reliable friend that helped me cope, and always stayed with me through thick and thin, day and night, each day and, wherever I happened to rest my head. My pen became my friend, my so called 'bestie'. Any pen would do. David Larbi, in his poem, Pen Friend, also explains why he too regards 'the pen' as his friend too as he could no longer rely on the family TV which had broken down. For me 'the pen' became a longed for, new-found and very precious friend. I loved to write, and I loved to read all kinds of books, especially folktales, and I really enjoyed memorising nursery rhymes as well create new rhyming poems.

Writing was fun because I could use my imagination to create any story I wanted to, or express my feelings in any way I could without being stopped. It 'freed' me up because when I was actually writing I had no time to think about anything that made me sad. I simply 'put on hold' all those awful feelings of loss and abandonment I had felt as a little girl. Writing helped me to stay happy!

However, writing, I soon discovered, in my younger years, was also a very lonely activity. For my thoughts and ideas to flow freely I did not want to be disturbed. I was happy to be in my own company even if this meant sometimes cutting myself off from people, from my friends and from those who took care of me. Whether writing a poem, a short story, a few lines of a song or an entry in my 'teen diary' the more I wrote the more 'freed up' I felt. Yet the more disconnected and lonelier I became. I craved to meet, share, discuss and perform my work with other girls and boys just like me who were just as crazy about writing as I was.

That did not happen until I was about twenty-four, in 1985, whilst studying for a degree in Sociology at Kingston Polytechnic. By now I was writing very little poetry but more factual stuff which you have to do as an 'undergraduate' (a university student). At least I had found some friends who liked writing just like me. Friends I could share and discuss my essays and opinions with about society. I had found some 'pen friends'.

I hope readers can now understand why wanting a friend or buddy to write with when I was a little girl partly inspired me to create WAPPY in years to come. Another reason for wanting to create a club for young writers is to do with having the privilege of getting to know a few young writers through the work I have been doing as a performance artiste and workshop facilitator in schools and heritage sites around London, from 1997 to 2008. Each time I had the chance to read through a child's poem, story or encountered their artwork, I really appreciated the effort this writer had made in conjuring up some meaningful words, sentences and images to grab my attention and other readers' attentions to experience a bit of, or all of his or her imaginary world.

This is more or less what happened in the case of Lindsay Warner, one of WAPPY's early members. I was in the home of Carolyn Warner, a friend I have known since starting at Hobbayne Primary. She showed me her daughter, Lindsay's poem, which had been published in 'Middlesex

Poets' by their local borough of Hounslow. As I read the poem of this very gifted 10-year-old, I expressed my delight to Lindsay, and, as her face lit up with a broad smile, I congratulated her on her achievement at being an author at such a young age. Almost at the same time another friend, Ifilia Francois, director of the Positive Awareness Charity in Acton, called me on my mobile. She asked if I would be interested in starting up a project which her organisation would happily support. She would help me to find volunteers and local grants if I had a project in mind.

I then experienced what can only be described as a 'Eureka moment' because it was from then onwards I knew I wanted to be part of a process that would help to inspire other youngsters in a group setting to write their own creative material, perform and showcase that creativity confidently, and to get that material published in a book, for those young writers who love reading books. I felt it was important to create or find opportunities for children and young people to get their literature 'out there' digitally through social media or as E books or in other ways. I was keen to help ignite, light up, the faces of young writers too. In other words, I wanted lots of young people to experience many more Eureka moments like me!!

Thus, in May 2008, WAPPY became part of Positive Awareness, and at the same time Ealing Council (Youth & Connexions Division) agreed to offer us a small grant to a run a summer holiday scheme. The first summer holiday project took place at the Lifeline Learning Academy in Hanwell from 29th July 2008 and ran until 18th August 2008. We recruited three volunteer workshop assistants and worked with nine young people (ages 11 to 14 years) who lived in the boroughs of Ealing, Brent, Hillingdon, and Hounslow. Our members met one afternoon a week for three weeks and were inspired by their peers, while guided too by me, to write poems and create a group story, which they showcased on the final day, in front of their families, sponsors and community supporters. Needless to say, for the first ever showcase the venue was jam-packed, and the group of nine thrilled the audience, which included publishers, Jessica and Eric Huntley from Bogle L'Ouverture Press, Nicole Moore from Shangwe, Verna Wilkins from Tamarind Books and Sue Cooke from Random House Children's Books. They displayed such a confidence that Sue Cook remarked after the event,

"I felt very privileged to be invited to attend the WAPPY showcase - and excited to hear the youngsters reading out their work, and clearly demonstrating such creativity and talent. The standard of writing was very high indeed - with a fantastic emphasis on each member being encouraged to develop their own individual 'voice'. As an editor within a large publishing house, I know how important it is to encourage new writers for the future and some of these young people showed definite potential to be among our next generation of published authors."

Sue Cook, Senior Editor, Random House Children's Books, 2008

WAPPY's First Final Showcase (19/09/08)
As I hope to show you below from the timeline of events starting from May 2008 right through to August 2018, our achievements have been phenomenal. Each chapter has been organised around various themes that matter to our writers, which were inspired by specific projects we have run over the decade. It's not surprising, given that we are such a diverse group, with children from so many different cultural and ethnic backgrounds, that the subject of 'belonging' and being of mixed-heritage is a big deal in the anthology. So too are the subjects of love, fear, and other emotions which come under the heading of 'Feelings'. Many of our contributors love animals, real and mythical ones and have re-worked traditional stories that feature animals, hence the reason for including 'Creatures Great and Small'.

The topic I think that has proved to be the most important and popular is 'friendships' which comes under the heading of 'Building Bridges', that WAPPY has delivered as three separate projects between 2013 to 2017 because of its popularity. The project has encouraged WAPPY members to work with their peers who were acquaintances and did not really 'hang out' with rather than friends. With the use of team-building and bridge building activities participants have developed new bonds and friendships with them. This way those who took part in Building Bridges were able to break down barriers and made strong friendships or simply worked well with someone new for that workshop they attended. Through playing games, writing, drama and artwork these youngsters built bridges and have written passionately about these experiences in that chapter.

Other themes in the anthology are included because WAPPY ran certain projects and workshops that were shaped by historical celebrations and global events such as the Bicentenary of Charles Dickens, London 12, (the Olympics), Bob Marley's 70th Birthday Anniversary, Bob Dylan's Nobel Prize for Literature Award, and the Christmas Festivity. In the case of Charles Dickens, under the guidance of artistic director and poet, Anjan Saha, and me, various writers who were inspired by his novel 'Hard Times', teamed up during a WAPPY session in January 2012 to create a group poem, entitled 'Hard Times It Just Is', which was performed at the Huntley Archives Conference, February 2012. That poem used phrases and ideas from Dickens to try to make sense of why the riots started in Tottenham (North London) on 6th August 2011 and spread across London (including Ealing) to other parts of England.

In contrast, for the Bob Marley and Bob Dylan projects, WAPPY ran poetry contests and prize-giving showcases and exhibitions, with the help of Ealing Libraries (then managed by the company, Carillion). We wanted to motivate those young people who took part in the workshops and/or researched these international iconic artists to produce high quality and inspirational poetry and understand how writing poems and songs can have a massive impact on the world.

On the other hand, Root To The Fruit, represents the local involvement of fifteen WAPPY members in a collaborative Heritage Lottery-funded Oral History Project. These writers described poetically their different experiences of being trained up as researchers by me and by the Black Cultural Archives in South London to interview ten African/Caribbean elders, who shared their 'Back Home' stories. They also spoke of how they adjusted to life in Ealing after their arrival from Africa or from the Caribbean and explained how they had contributed to the Ealing community from the 1950s to the 1970s.

There is also a chapter that embraces the deep thoughts our writers have expressed on some subjects that even adults often struggle to deal with, like the death of a sibling, the fear of losing a parent, experiencing conflict in war-torn Syria, being bullied, having to become a 'different person' in order to grow inside, coping with disability, and speaking out against young people who get themselves involved in gangs and crimes.

It was also important to include a chapter on short, funny poems (rhyming and non-rhyming) and limericks which have been created by our younger writers (ages 4-8). Some of these children dictated what they wanted us to write because they found writing a little too difficult or were simply too tired after a long day at school. Some of them sketched and painted pictures, which I and other workshop staff encouraged them to write down what their artwork meant to them. These 'Short, Sweet and Smiley' writings are meant to make younger readers smile and laugh. However, as they are rather simple and different in structure, and easy to learn off by heart, we hope this chapter will prove to be a useful resource, especially for teachers of KS1 (reception, Year 1, 2, 3, and 4) students in primary schools, who are working to address changes brought about by former Education Secretary Minister Michael Gove. He recommended that children as young as five must learn and recite poetry in the new national curriculum for schools in England from 2015.

Another chapter features stories, some fairly long and some very short ones, and some with artwork by our younger writers, whose sketches also help us to make sense of their narratives.

You will find touching tributes dedicated to famous 'movers and shakers', by this I mean men and women who have touched the lives of some of our writers on a personal or not so personal but global level. The final chapter, 'Wonderful World of WAPPY' I think is probably the most important, because we hear from some of the first and early members who started with WAPPY in the summer holidays of 2008 and 2009. Now adults who are between 18 and 24 years old, they reflect back on the ways in which WAPPY has helped them in their individual lives. Some also tell us what they are doing today.

Believe it or not, I have only provided you with a snippet of what is to come. The poems, short-stories and artwork will take you on an historical journey, back and forth, and each contributor, from the youngest of 4 to the oldest of 24 years, has his and her own unique narrative to share. They are very equipped to comment on our world as they see it. A world, incidentally, which may at times seem very different from the Wonderful World of WAPPY! Indeed, some refer to WAPPY as "family!"

Grace Quansah
WAPPY founder & Director

WAPPY Timeline

May 2008, WAPPY partnered with the Positive Awareness Charity and received £750 Ealing Council funding to run summer holiday workshops and a Final Showcase (Lifeline Learning Centre, W7).

2008-2013, performances at local/national events (e.g. WAPPY Showcases, 2008-2013, Acton Carnival 09, The Huntley Archives Conferences, 2010-2014, London Maze, Guildhall, 2010, Ealing Apprenticeships Awards Ceremony, 2013, Junior Authors Writers Conference, Guildford, 2014, with flautist, Keith Waithe, Ealing Jazz Festival, 2014, Grenadian Sunshine Foundation, 2015.

2009 (August), for the summer holidays WAPPY now catered for young people between the ages 10 to 14 years; and partnered with Ealing Literary Festival for 13 members to take part in Acton Carnival procession as well as perform in the Cultural Quarter of the Carnival in Acton Park (June).

The 2009, summer workshops attracted increased numbers, and participants created poems including Michael Jackson tributes, following his death on 22nd June, which were performed at the Lifeline Academy (August). Akuba was joined by local artists, Aamasade Shepnekhi, 'TUUP' ('The Unprecedented, Unorthodox Preacher') and Jojo Yates for the 'Anansi and the Golden Box' collaborative performance.

August 2009, Capacity funding, sponsored by IT consultant, Cheryl Burke, enabled WAPPY to have its first web site. Training was provided for its members and staff (February 2010) and Akuba took over as its administrator.

2010, Georgiana Jackson-Callen became Poetry Winner of the Youth Relief Talent Competition organised by the 'Thank U Charity', led by Sally Baffour. Georgiana also created WAPPY's debut DVD.

June 2010, we designed signage for Acton Carnival.

2010, 2013 & 2014, we produced inspirational postcards and posters with Leanne Creatives.

October 2010, eight members were published in A Lime Jewel to raise funds for the Haiti earthquake survivors.

October 2010 to October 2011, fifteen trained members interviewed ten African-descended elders for the Root to The Fruit, Oral History, Heritage Lottery Project.

February 2011, thirty-five members from seven London boroughs had their poems, stories and artwork published in the LMA funded anthology, The Soul of a Child, by Bogle L'Ouverture Press.

May 2012, five WAPPY poets were published in Sweet Beats for Keats, Maureen Roberts and Benjamin Zephaniah, (Eds.), following their participation in the 'A Haven for Words' workshop run by Akuba in 2011.

July - August 2012, WAPPY ran summer holiday (Olympics 2012 - themed), Help a Capital Child funded workshops in Ealing Central Library, which inspired poetry and artwork, plus a Community Games/London 12 Day, St Dunstan's Church (W3), funded by Pro-Active, West London (Brunel University).

October 2012, for the Charles Dickens Bicentenary, with Ealing Libraries and Ealing Autumn Festival 2012, and Help a Capital Child funding, WAPPY showcased 'Hard Times, It Just Is', a poetic reinterpretation. Eighteen members performed it at the Huntley Archives Conference in February 2013.

December 2012, we ran an 'Anansi' - themed workshop, which led to seven WAPPY works being published in Anansesem, January ending 2013.

March 2013, with West Twyford Youth & Community Project, we ran the 'Building Bridges' Project (Brent), culminating in the production of inspirational designed cards, a Community Games Day, creative writing and a showcase.

December 2012, WAPPY won £10K from The Big Lottery (Awards for All), to help it develop from a project to an organisation. Through Kyria Consulting Ltd 11 volunteers were trained in community leadership and gained accreditation

April 2013, more funding from Help A Capital Child enabled the 'My Favourite Book' club to run spring/summer term 2013. Also, eighteen members (5 to 14 years) had their works accepted for publication on The Scrumbler web site.

June 2013, WAPPY became a social enterprise, and a registered company; autonomous of Positive Awareness. We appointed 5 trustees, John Durston, Carolyn Warner, Dr. Graham Shaw, Anjan Saha and Grace Quansah (Akuba).

August 2013, Summer holiday programme included the 3rd Community Games at London Network church (Acton) Some Nostalgia Steel Pan Players played.

August 2013, Eric Huntley and Sally Baffour became Patrons of WAPPY. Staff, parents and invited guests at Hanwell Library celebrated WAPPY's 5-year Reunion & Rebirth anniversary; with WAPPY acts.

February 2014, following the passing of Jessica Huntley (WAPPY's ardent fan), 13 October 2013, eight WAPPY members pay tribute to her memory with poetry readings and music at the 9th Huntley Archives Conference (LMA).

September 2014, WAPPY & Hot Key Books hosted a public event with Benjamin Zephaniah. Members, Cassius Callen-Jackson, Honey Ryder & 'Jai Ellis' entertained him and 15 members interviewed him about his novel, Terror Kid, Ealing Central Library.

February 2015, for The Story So Far Arts Council funded project, some WAPPY writers performed original poetry and read from The Soul of a Child at its launch (Acton Library).

April 2015, WAPPY partnered with Walpole Park and On the Ball FC to run a Charity Football Match and Games Day.

April - May 2015, WAPPY & CCS Libraries/Ealing hosted the Bob Marley 70th Anniversary Tribute, at Ealing Central Library. Works from the workshops were emailed to Rita Marley in Ghana, Brenda Powell from the Rita Marley Foundation thanked WAPPY.

June 2015, Bob Marley poetry contest winner, Jessica Howard, Gerda Kleinberga and Akuba performed original poetry for the Women of the Year Awards ceremony, organised by Ealing Women's Forum, Walpole Park in Ealing.

October 2015, WAPPY & CCS Libraries/Ealing hosted a book launch of Mame Nwia-Amah: Maisa & Sara Abed interviewed author, Esther Ackah.

November 2015, Khesumaba Jess/KA Filmworks visited a WAPPY workshop at Ealing Central Library, Unpacking That Trunk/Marcus Garvey (Ealing Central Library) to film writers and staff in action for a Marcus Garvey-inspired film.

April 2016, we ran the Great WAPPY Bake Off in St. Dunstan's Church to raise funds. Great British Bake Off 2013 runner up, Ruby Tandoh, donated her book 'Crumb' and Australian author, Wendy Sharpe donated her co-edited book with Annabel Crabb, 'Special Delivery'.

December 2017, WAPPY & CCS Libraries/Ealing hosted the Forever Young Bob Dylan Showcase, following primary & secondary school age research workshops to produce prize-winning poetry and artwork. Runaway Entertainment, producers of the Dylan-inspired West-End musical, 'Girl from the North Country', donated theatre tickets, and CDs for the literary competition and show-case; actor, Jack Shalloo visited the Forever Young Showcase and was interviewed by 10 WAPPY members (ages 5-14).

March 2018, WAPPY members, staff and trustees who participated in 'What I Like About Ealing,' workshop (July 2017) featured in the 'A Film About Ealing', led by ARTification and funded by the Arts Council.

March 2018, WAPPY won £4,500 Near Neighbours funding to run its popular Building Bridges Project (ages 4-16 years) at St. Dunstan's (April-June 2018). Forty-eight from the WAPPY community saw the School of Rock; seventeen workshop participants created inspirational postcards and personalised inspirational T-shirts; and a group of 6 children visited the Youth Symposium, Spring Festival at the LMA where 5 members performed their literature, inspired by a Box of Akuba's artefacts. They also interviewed Lindsay Warner, award-winning writer, former 2009 veteran WAPPY member & current volunteer.

July 2018, WAPPY parent, Joan Jackson-Callen, MBE, took a group of WAPPY members, some trustees and parents to view the Michael Jackson- inspired, 'On the Wall' exhibition at the National Portrait Gallery.

August 2018, WAPPY organised a Family & Friends Picnic & Rounders day at Gunnersbury Park (W3);16 WAPPY members (ages 4 to 14) got together with our families and staff to play Rounders and have a picnic. Some young people created new writing pieces and received their personalised T Shirts.

November 2018, WAPPY is funded by Arts Council England (ACE) to publish 'Wonderful World of WAPPY' & host the 10 Year Anniversary event.

Ten years on, developing and encouraging new creative writers for the future through interactive reading, performance storytelling and poetry, problem-solving, teamwork, creative media, arts, crafts and construction activities, remain at the heart of what WAPPY does. However, we also provide opportunities now for our members to interview authors and other key figures in the arts, as well as offer training and volunteering opportunities for students, the unemployed and others who would like to improve their future.

Today, internationally acclaimed Dub poet and social commentator, Professor, Benjamin Zephaniah, describes WAPPY as the 'United Nations of Children'. We have worked with hundreds of young people of different ethnic groups and colours, classes, creeds and creative abilities, from within the Ealing borough, and across London, including from the boroughs of Camden, Islington, Croydon, Hammersmith & Fulham, Harrow, Hillingdon, Hounslow, Brent and also Guildford, Surrey.

We have also expanded our provision by offering afterschool term-time workshops, by lowering the registration age so that now 4-year olds can join us, and by raising the age limit to 18 years. The aim is to help students with their school studies and help them progress from primary school to high school, and on to college and university and work, at various stages.

From humble beginnings in 2008, WAPPY gained funding from the Big Lottery in November-ending 2012 after a successful bid, to train its then eleven volunteers to do a Community Leadership course with accreditation. This subsequently led to WAPPY reconstituting itself (changing how it organised itself) to form a Board of Trustees and became a registered company, limited by guarantee in June 2013. As a newly formed social enterprise, this meant we became completely separate from Positive Awareness. We always grateful to PA for its support.

The title of the anthology, 'Wonderful World of WAPPY', was created by a group of WAPPY participants in 2012. The book represents the thoughts, feelings, words, ideas, images, visualisations, hopes, aspirations and inspirations of more than a hundred young writers and several young illustrators who have participated in one or more WAPPY workshops and/or related community activities since its birth in 2008.

I believe the writers' poetry and short-stories, with and without illustration speak for themselves, so it is not my intention to give too much more away! By bringing alive and sharing the WAPPY literature, with younger, older, and mature readers, that magical feeling I and many other WAPPY associates have experienced when reading these extraordinary, heartfelt poems and stories, is generated. And we know that we are truly celebrating the wonderful world of WAPPY over ten magnificent years!

They deserve to be heard and they deserve to be authors.

Enjoy!

Grace Quansah *(Akuba)*

All About WAPPY

Artwork by Athena Ioannou
2018

HAPPY IN WAPPY

I am happy!
But why am I happy?
And I think it's WAPPY.
So happy because I'm in WAPPY!
Too happy because I'm in WAPPY!

YES I'M HAPPY
BECAUSE I'M
IN .... WAPPY!

Marianne Deutsch-Bruce (8) 2014

I love WAPPY

I love WAPPY
Because we Play Games,
We Write Poems,
Draw and Do Acting

Wonderful
Amazing
Powerful
Poetry
Yeepy

Yasmine Fetit (6) 2014

WAPPY

I like WAPPY because it is fun
Because we do poems and write
We get sweets, water and go home
It is fun!

Rana Omar (6) 2014

WAPPY Helps Us Succeed

WAPPY has changed us
We were so shy
We never thought that we could succeed
But look what we have achieved!
Poems, drama and artwork too,
Even though we claimed we had no clue,
This isn't a lie but is the truth!

Izoje Owaka (15) and Effie Quansah-George (13) 2017

We Love WAPPY

WAPPY is here
So, friends are near
We know how to rhyme
As we have the time
Even though that's all we know
We're the stars of the show
At WAPPY!

Seren Sim (11) 2017

Building Bridges

Artwork by Acquaye McCalman

A Few Words of Bridges

Bridges of Teamwork
Creative
Unique
Building
Under or Over
Through or Across
Shelter or Bridge
No matter what Shape or Size
Colour or Style,
To make a Bridge
You need a Work of Team!

Effie Quansah-George (10) 2014

A Friendship Like a Bridge

You have to make a friendship
Like a bridge,
Strong and trustworthy,
Make your bridge strong
With friendship.

Don't let your bridge fall,
Build it into strong foundation
The weaker the friendship
The quicker it will sink

Ivy Oppong (11) 2014

A Stormy Day

Jay was at the park,
There was no one to be seen.
Swings winding round and round,
As fast as a racing car,
He really wanted to scream!

Branches and leaves were rustling,
Trees were falling down like a bowling ball.
He heard a zap of lightening,
He really wanted to bawl!

Lights around flashed on and off,
Thunder roared through the clash of clouds.
BOOM! SLAP! ZAP! WALLA! CLASH!
Jay really wanted to run,
Because he wasn't having any fun!

Suddenly, the swings winded to a steady halt,
No more trees crashed to the floor.
The thunder switched off, while the lightening disappeared,
Guess who appeared?
EVERYONE!
Jay really wanted to PLAY!

Mark Mwangi (7) 2014

Building a Friendship

Hi!
I am Mariam,
I might be small,
I might be unique,
But my friends like me the way I am,
And when I need help,
They are always there for me,
Like I will always be there for them,
And together we build a bridge.
That's what friends are for.
Therefore, I love my friends,
And the bridges we build together.

Mariam Allawi (6) 2014

Fake Friends

You see your 'friends',
They say mean things to you,
But you stay cool.
When you see them upset,
You say nice things to them.

Nazir Gentry (10) 2014

Friends

When I think about the friends I have,
I kind of feel quite glad,
I should respect them all.
Without all of them,
I would hardly have a friend
They make me happy when I'm sad.

One day I walked through the park,
I saw my friend,
She looked at me and said,
"It's really you Seren!
I haven't seen you for a while!"

I think I know why I haven't seen you for a week,
You're nice, you're not a freak!"
That's what Mary said.
I shouldn't believe people who say I don't like you.

Seren Sim (7) 2014

Friendship

You may
Break my Bridge
But you will not
Break my Friendship
And that's why we're a team.

Work all together!
If you don't like that,
Then live your life
The way you want it!
You may
Break my Bridge
But you will not
Break my Friendship.

Imara Turney (10) 2014

Make Yourself Happy

If you are sad
Don't give up
Make yourself happy,
Play with someone else
And say,
"I want to play with you!"

Yasmine Fetit (6) 2014

Stretch of Happiness

The bridge is part of a city called London.
Its aim is to at least prove,
That it's building up trust.
Therefore, the bridge is going to show its capability,
That it is full of self-esteem,
And can build up strong abilities for other people,
Who are going through a rough time at the moment.

The bridge can also build
Mega happiness, partially
Because it has got that sense about it,
When you walk upon it
And feel that stretch of happiness.

Savannah Wight (13) 2013

The Bridge of Life

One father. One Mother.
Many problems. Many moments.
Unsturdy bridge. Slowly falling.
Trying to be fixed. Being mended.
At the end, the bridge stays strong.

THE BRIDGE OF LIFE
Can make one. Can break one.
The journey may be long and daunting,
But in the end, all is always well.

Ivy Oppong (14) 2018

The Wish Bridge

Hold the wish on your tongue
As you cross the invisible bridge
On the far side.

Let the wish go first,
for what the bridge cannot hear, cannot fall.

Between here and now,
Between me and you is the word 'bridge'.

The wish will appear
In one burst.
It will go when it reaches.

Tell me when it will show.

Pierre Ikong (11) 2018

What are friends?

Friends are people who stay by your side,
When you need help they are there.
When you cry
They wipe your tears
When you have things that you can't tell anyone
They are there to help out.

Marwah Nabizada (10) 2014

Christmas

A Soul of the Lord

Christmas means so much to me,
Because I am a Christian
And a soul of the Lord.

I do not care if I wake up
On Christmas morning with no presents
Because I spend time with God
And my family.

My soul takes control over my love!

Shelay Busby (10) 2012

Christmas is Asleep

Christmas! Christmas!
Why do you never wake up?
You always snore all morning and night,
And make people think … 'what is it?'
But when people try to wake up Mr Christmas,
He snores even louder!
Snow! Snow! Wake up!
Help me wake up Christmas!
When is Christmas going to wake up…When!

Majd Mansour (8) 2012

Countdown to Christmas!

There are 31 days in December,
From 14th to Christmas Eve
Are 4 more days.
We all countdown to
CHRISTMAS!!!!

Emma Boundy (6) 2012

Most Favourite Time of Year

Christmas is a time
For celebrating the Saviour's birth.
Families gather up
To exchange presents to one another.

Christmas is my most favourite time of year.
Every year I give money
To the world,
People around the world.

My school does a fundraising scheme
And all the children give fruits,
A home-made necklace and a scarf
We then put it in a box
To be sent off!

Ida Mwangi (11) 2012

Shining Star

When I look up on the sky,
I see a star shinning bright.
Then I look to the left
And see Santa shouting, "Merry Christmas!"

I see a flashing red light in the sky,
I watch the red light flashing everywhere.
Soon I see Santa with his red cheeks,
And a big smile on his face,
But soon I fall sleepy
And fall into a deep, deep sleep.

Leika Boundy (8) 2012

The Jolly Holly

Christ was born on Christmas day to save us from our sins
Herod, thy horrid of the time had a discouraging,
    disturbing plan in his mind
Right hand of thy Father is where thee shall one day
    sit this baby boy, Jesus
Infinite in a manger, his first place to sleep.
Sitting down on a stack of hay, Mary and Joseph
    say "Shepherds were guided."
To see this day, that is so sweet, together with
    animals in a manger you lay.
My Saviour, Jesus Christ, was brought gifts by three
    kings of old.
Angels sing, "Hallelujah, Hallelujah," to the new born King!
So we finish knowing the real meaning of Christmas
    day, to give thanks,
To our Lord God for the birth of his only son, our Saviour,
    Christ our Lord, Jesus.

T-Khai James-Palmer-Wahome-Kellehey (9) 2017

What Christmas Means to Me

Christmas is the most beautiful time of the year
Because when I wake up in the morning,
I see presents stacked up like building blocks,
And sometimes I wonder,
If they come by magic!

All the beautiful and colourful wrapping paper,
Shinning in the sunlight.
When it is time to open the presents,
I imagine all the colourful paper,
Flying in all directions!

Emilia Ferreira (12) 2012

Creatures Great and Small

Artwork by Acquaye McCalman
2012

Anansi

There is Anansi
Staring at me,
I mean, look at those eyes,
Big and scary.

Look at it sitting,
Sitting so silent
So evil,
Like it's thinking,
Thinking too much.

I try to look away,
Forget it's even there.
I try so hard but
It's just …. Wait……Where?

I sometimes sit and wonder,
I wonder if they get scared
I mean just like us
By their friends, are they dared?

Dared to show their faces,
I mean do they have a brain?
Do they go school
Just like me?

Do they have a life?
In their own world
Do they have friends,
And time to be sorry?

Anyway, back to Anansi
Wait! Where could it be!
Oh, please don't!
It's right above me!!!

Sonam Ubhi (15) 2012

An Anansi Warning

People think you are scary,
But I find you are sweet.
They say you bring me good luck
Like an apple falling from a tree.

Black, brown and scary,
And sometimes, thin, skinny and hairy.

I see you in your web
Spinning silk and tales,
Leaving mysterious words of different trails,
Sharing stories all around the world.

Fiction or fact?
Anansi… please cut me some slack!

Effie Quansah-George (8) 2012

Billy Goat Adventures

Breath as foul as an ogre's snot.
Into the hills he runs,
Licking his lips as the mountain fog clears.
Leaving his home to find fresh grass,
Gently placing his hoofs among the freshly grown trees.

Only frightened by a lion,
Along the bridge he trots alone.
The bridge collapses and the goat falls,
But he survives among the glittering riverbed.
He has fallen, but he will arise.

Seren Sim (11) 2018

Dragon

Once there lived a dragon
Who was mean,
He ate people.
One day he helped a person,
He felt good
He didn't eat people any more.

Shangwe Thomas (6) 2013

Fly Away My friend

Fly away my friend
It's night
Your natural time of flight

Fly away my friend
And you'll fly in the sky beneath the moon light

Fly away my friend
Flap your beautiful, brown wings to the sky
But lie in the day on your leaf

Fly away my friend
And don't stay till May

Fly away my friend
And keep safe till the end of your life

Fly away my friend
And keep strong till dawn

Fly away my friend
And keep safe till the end of your life

Gerda Kleinberga (10) 2014

The Hare and the Tortoise

This is a story to pass down,
This is a story to share.
Now we will begin the tale
Of the Tortoise and the Hare

In the middle of the forest
On the dot of Harrowmill Chase,
Hundreds and hundreds of fellow animals
Were preparing for the annual race.

The Hare was rather boastful
And as he puffed up his chest,
Proclaimed he was the fastest
Much faster than the rest.

The Tortoise, he was humble,
He was extremely slow,
But he never stopped going,
"Because there's a long way to go."

The Tortoise and the Hare lined
At the start of the race,
Max's heart was beating fast
But Toby's at the normal pace.

Then there was a BANG! BANG! BANG!
The three gunshots were heard
Max zoomed round the pathway
So fast he blew down a bird!

The Tortoise started his steady stroll
Across the yellow path.
He knew he must not rush,
Best be steady than fast

The Hare stopped halfway through the race
To chatter with his fans.
He played pink pong all by himself,
To hear a round of clapping hands.

The Hare stopped by the pit stop
And bought himself a Freezie.
He sat down on a haystack
And said, "Winning is easy."

The Tortoise just walked past him,
Because he was sleep.
Just then he wondered
Why people count sheep.

Toby crawled near the finished line
When the Hare woke up
"He hasn't passed me yet," he thought,
"I'll go refill my cup."

Toby caught hold of the ribbon,
The checkered line he passed.
He was filled with happiness,
He'd won a race at last!

When the Hare walked past,
To expect the roaring crowds,

But all there was to greet him,
Was the shinning cloud.
The trophy went to Toby,
With cookie and ice-cream inside.
The Hare just watched and stared.
He'd been overcome with pride.
Now here's the lesson
Beneath the fable skins,
The moral of this story?
Slow and steady wins!

Maia Hicks (9) 2014

The Three Little Kids

Once upon a time, there were three little kids,
Who were named Apples, Pomegranates and Figs
They lived in a house not far from the woods
And secretly smuggled prohibited goods

When she found out about their illegal escapades,
She said, "I've seen nothing like this in all of my days!"
Since you need some discipline inside you,
I'm shipping you off to Timbuktu

Their situations seemed scarier,
When they succumbed to malaria,
Their temperatures were rocketing, their vision was hazy
And their doctor, a witch doctor, turned out to be crazy

The witch doctor immediately called for his comrade, The fox,
Whose methods always worked although they were Unorthodox

His tail swished happily, his eyes began to evilly gleam
As he set his mind to a felonious scheme

The kids were lying lazily on the floor,
When they heard three knocks at the door
Fox said, "I'm here to make your dreams come true
All you have to do is trust me - will you?

Apples and Pomegranates went straight away
Ignoring Figs' pleas to make them stay
He quickly put on some clever disguises
To shadow them and halt the impending crisis

Hastily, he set off to stalk the fox
Wearing sunglasses, a false nose and a wig of golden locks
He followed him absolutely everywhere
Until he found his secret lair

Figs saw his brothers had been knocked out with Sleeping drugs
They lay limply on the table like short, fat slugs
He scanned the room for a place to stay
And decided to crouch under the table where his Brothers lay

He noticed the drugs were in a leather pouch,
Which rested on the arm of the witch doctor's couch
Figs glanced at the drugs which he wanted to pocket
But he needed to get them as fast as a rocket

He put the drugs into the witch doctors cup
Which the evil man was about to gulp up
He drank it up in three seconds flat
And then he collapsed right on the mat

The fox looked at the witch doctor on the floor
Then he glanced back at the wide-open door
He was nearly at the door; he could nearly touch the hinges
But his progress was halted with two drug - filled Syringes
And that is the story of the three little kids
Apples, Pomegranates and clever little Figs.

Paul Larbi (9) & Daniel Larbi (12) 2011

The Three Bears and Goldilocks

In a town called Acton
Once upon a time,
Lived three furry bears
All was far from fine.

Daddy, Mummy
And Baby Bear too,
Were so very naughty
What could grandma do?

Grandma had enough
Threw them all out,
Bowling down the high street,
Screamed and messed about!

Zookeeper spots them.
Thought they had escaped
He caught them in the Mall,
They tried to buy some plates.

The bears broke out,
Headed for New Forest
Boy, they were so happy
"We have found a little cottage!"

Baby Bear put a stick
Through the letter box,
They were so surprised
To find the door unlocked.

The house was Goldilocks,
Her name was on the door,
They entered very quietly
Softly on their paws.

"A hand-baked chocolate cake,"
Temptation was too much.
Baby bear could not resist
And stuffed his mouth right up!

They looked in all the rooms,
Goldilocks was snoring,
Baby opened up his mouth
Then he started growling.

Goldilocks woke up
They gave her quite a fright!
She locked them in a cupboard,
There they had no light

The little one began to cry
"Oh Baby don't be sad."
Goldilocks let them out
Then the bears were glad.

The bears and Goldilocks
Shared a bowl of porridge
They read some books
To improve their knowledge.

Leika Boundy (7), Effie Quansah-George (7)
and Grace Simons (6) 2011

Deep Thinking

Wappy Workshop 2009

Alone

You can be alone.
But just because you're alone,
It doesn't mean you have to be lonely.
The two words may sound the same
But are completely different in reality.
Just because I'm alone,
It doesn't mean I'm looking for a friend
Or a way to be less lonely.
I'm a human being.
We need to be alone sometimes.

Seren Sim (11) 2018

A New Day's Coming

A new day's coming.
We can't wait!
It's a school day,
And we don't care.
We have fun at school too!

Then the new day ends
And we are going to bed.
Bye Bye, Night Night,
Then turn out the light.

Shangwe Thomas (6) 2013

A Rainbow

A rainbow is magic
Magic that flows
Flows like a river
A river filled with gold
Gold from a leprechaun
A leprechaun with a clover
A clover for luck
Luck from God
God with a promise
A promise never to be broken.

Renée Dawkins (10) 2013

Arriving in Swotsville

When I arrived in Swotsville
I thought I was in another planet.
This strange and mysterious place
Pulled me towards it like a magnet.

School is three centuries long!
It couldn't get any faster,
And if you get even the tiniest thing wrong,
You're straight to the Headmaster.

There are very strange people,
They wouldn't even laugh.
They don't find a joke funny
School has taken away their humorous self.

I don't like this place
It's what no one expects,
But what I'm anxious about is,
What will happen next!

Maia Hicks (9) 2013

Black is the New Black

Black is the new black,
And us blacks we fight back.
Think about the old times,
As sour as lime.
But as sweet as honey,
As light as a bunny.
Back in history,
Some find a mystery.
White on black and black on white,
Some think that is not right.
But all changed.
New world,
New life.
We can be,
Lawyers, ballerinas,
Singers, actors.
Now we have a chance of winning X-factors.
Blacks have good jobs,
None of those big bad mobs.
We all live as one,
Hope all the bad things have been done.
One last thing from me to you,
Just do the best you can DO!
Because you can.

Kyra Nelson (9) 2016

Brain and Heart

I walked through the park,
That's when I met a heart.
I walked away but it followed me.

I went through the door,
That's when I saw more.
In the corner of my eyes I saw a brain.
I was so shocked that I walked to my room.
The heart and the brain had both followed me.

I was so furious that I went,
The brain was so fed up that it had said,
 "Who cares?"
The heart was astonished that she had said,
"You do!"

Marwah Nabizada (10) 2014

Dear Syria

I am writing to thank you

You inspired me to smile
You inspired me to aim
You inspired me to laugh
You inspired me to dream
You inspired me to shine

But most of all

YOU INSPIRED ME TO LOVE

Julia Baramo (11) 2012

Fight For My Freedom

A world full of pain and betrayal,
Sacrifice and injustice,
War and dispute.
I fight for my freedom
While the hands grab me.

I'm so young, yet so unlucky.
My heart beats,
My eyes shut as I start to lose my grip.
I am in the enemy's hands.

My spine shivers,
Fingers twitch,
I fight for my freedom
While the hands grab me.

Sarai Aidoo-Richardson (14) 2018

Gangster

Gangster, gangster
You think you're So Cool!
Your pants hanging low
Gold chains. You Fools!

Robbing from shops,
Committing crime.
Just listen because
Now is the time,
To change your life.
It ain't about looks,
The money or status.
So, put down the phone
And pick up the books!

I used to be afraid of Gangsters,
Not going to lie,
But now I hold my head up high.
You wouldn't act like this,
If you used your brains,
So, stop being vain
Because if you believe,
You will succeed.

That was a Wake-Up Call
From Me to You!
In other words,
Change.
Change for a better you!

Effie-Quansah-George (11) 2015

Girls

Good as any boy, tough and strong
Immaculate as any living being on the planet
Rustles and tussles to get on their way
Like a saber-tooth tiger in the present day
So now I come down to say "women rule, women are cool, down with the men!"

T-Khai James-Palmer-Wahome-Kellehey (10) 2018

Humble Whispers

I hear your humble whispers,
I feel your soft touch,
You understand me when others can't.
At times here in spirit when things are rough.

At times when I am despondent or confused,
I don't know what to do.
I am never truly lonely
Because, Alez you are with me,
Through and Through.

So, though my sweet brother you went
And flew away without a warning,
I feel I know you.
It may seem strange to say.

Sometimes I hear my mother cry,
She thinks I do not hear,
I guess those tears are healing tears,
Which will last years and years.

I often wonder, "Why or Why
Did you have to die so young?"
I always ask myself this question
Am I so wrong?

Maybe we just have to accept the Creator's way,
For he guides us each and every day.
So, my brother,
How are you today?

Centelia Tuitt-Walker (13) 2017, Contest Winner

I Am Afraid of Blank Paper

The teacher told me that I should write,
A poem on a piece of paper so white,
First came a shiver,
And then came a quiver,

I am afraid of blank paper.
I am afraid of blank paper yes me,
It might jeopardise my chance of a 5b,
It's not that I'm lazy,
Or a little bit crazy,
I am afraid of blank paper.

I am afraid of blank paper, it's not a lie,
Blank paper is more than meets the eye,
The test is so daunting,
And the paper is haunting,
I am afraid of blank paper.

I am afraid of blank paper don't jeer,
I'm mortified enough by my foolish fear,
Though paper is so bare,
It gives me a scare,
I am afraid of blank paper.

I am afraid of blank paper all right,
I know that blank paper doesn't bite,
But it is so intimidating,
And very humiliating,
It's just,
I am afraid of blank paper.

Honey Rider (11) 2014

Honey Ryder originally wrote, 'I'm Afraid of Blank Paper', for Christ The Saviour CofE Primary School's Poetry Slam, which she won in 2013. She performed it at Ealing Central Library (West London) during a special event, organised, by WAPPY in partnership with Hot Key Books and Cultural Communities Solutions (Ealing) for Benjamin Zephaniah to promote his new title, 'Terror Kid'.

The photo was taken by Duane Jay.

Just Society's Way

Aimlessly strolling she peers
Into each shop that takes her fancy.
Expensive clothes and brand-new shoes.
I hope to catch her eye.

But I am just a charity shop.
I am the one that offers used goods,
At dirt cheap prices.
I am the one that people think
Will reduce your status upon entrance.

But now I focus on my appearance and
Force a smile and keep my doors open wide,
And as I watch her freely enter an overpriced shop,
The same way one would enter their home,
I angrily wonder why she will never treat me
like home.

And then, sadly, I realise,
That she is searching for something.
Something that her friends will not judge her in.
Something that will not look too cheap.
But if she could hear me,
She would know that this is society's way
Of controlling her every move.
Through overpriced clothes and judgemental friends.

Renée Dawkins (15) 2017

Life

Planting something,
Giving birth to something,
Makes life go on forever,
Even in heaven.

Dying makes life halt,
But even if someone dies
Someone else's life might start.

Shangwe Thomas (7) 2014

Life Cycle

You start like a small seed in
Mummy's tummy.
Then grow into a
Chubby and round baby.

Next, a child, playing and learning
In primary school.
Soon after you're a teenager.

WOW! As you think you're growing taller.

Now, an independent adult,
Working and cooking for your family.

Finally, an elder,
With many respects
But at some point,
We become ancestors.

Effie Quansah-George (10) 2013

Life Story

Life is very busy and makes me quite dizzy
I have four siblings that make me extremely whizzy,
Friends are important, but I treasure family more,
Even members of my family who I don't adore!

School is cool but has loads of rules
Though be careful not to be the fool
Or you'll get excluded
Roar, snore, crack, lack, and you'll be sitting at the back
Yawn and you'll spawn in detention until dawn

T-Khai James-Palmer-Wahome-Kellehey (9) 2017

Look into My Eyes

Do not look at me, make your judgment
And walkaway.
I am not an open book.
Look deep in to my eyes,
I'm different,
My eyes are as deep as the Dead Sea.
My eyes tell her a story,
A beautiful one.

You will see my ups and downs,
My laughs and cries.
Just promise never to judge from your first sight,
For what you thought could be different.
Look deep into her eyes.

Everyone has a story as big as the Sahara.
As you sail among the stars,
Study each one before you say
Your last words.

Look deep into their eyes...

Maisa Abed (12) 2014

Love and Peace

Love is contagious if you have it,
Peace is a wonderful Christian value,
That everybody should have.
If you can dream it, then you can be it.

Love and peace, two forces so powerful,
So powerful, hate can't break through.
Don't listen to people who will hold you back,
As they could ruin your career.

Do what you must to fulfil your life,
And become the person you want to be.
Racism, discrimination and homophobic remarks are strong,
But together love and peace are stronger.

Christian Ferguson-Dawkins (11) 2017

Mirror

She comes to me daily,
And gazes into my face.
I reflect her truthfully,
Rewarded only with tears and anger.

She wants me to lie in reflection
I cannot tell a lie,
I remain loyal, always waiting for her,
Always reflecting what I see.

Sometimes, I move with her to the outside world.
She uses a façade, so easily seen through.
We return home together and she gazes into my face,
I reflect misery, loneliness and frustration.

I've known her for so long, loyal to her,
Her pain is my pain, I feel her sadness,
I smell her sweet scent as she breathes on me,
And feel her as she strokes, checking with reflection.

She comes to me again, seeking her reflection
I feel her growing agitation and anger.
She screams in denial, shaking me about,
But it's not my fault, I cannot tell a lie.

Lindsay Warner (11) 2009

My Success Criteria - Self Esteem

You started off like a seed.
All you need is for it to be freed
Encouragement, confidence, self-esteem will help succeed.

Make your way up the ranks
Until you find yourself at the top of the pack
Then you will clearly see self-esteem powers all of us, don't you see?

Self-esteem powers all of us don't you see?
So let it free for you and me,
Believe me because I know what I mean.
You know I'm right because this is the truth.
Then you'll make the most of your youth
Then you'll see the world differently
From the height above all of the trees

Imagine you're a little lion
Lying down on the floor by yourself.
All you want to do is a big roar
To clearly show that your esteem's not on the floor.
With a little luck the roar will appear
Then you will believe that you don't have fear.

With this high self-esteem
Let your gifts fly away with the stream
Let them soar
Let them never hit the floor
Let them never hit the floor
Then you'll finally get the score.

Keep success high and failures low.
Follow this and go with the flow.
Stick to this path and you will see
You are becoming the best person you can possibly be.
With these results you will clearly see,
Yourself growing continuously.

Think about me, for example,
Rapping here for you.
Do you see me turning me all blue?
The answer is "no" because my self-esteem is high.
Be just like me and you'll see your dreams fly.

All these gifts will call
More people to notice you.
And you will process this information
Then clearly find the clue.
High self-esteem and sharing your gifts
Is the best way to show the real you.

And then you'll be the best person you can possibly be
Now don't you all completely agree?

Kai-ern Thompson (16) 2018

My Life Is A Journey

My life is a journey, so is yours,
It's not a story,
So I don't have to explain my past.
All I care about
Is the present.
Presents, presents all year round,
Loving the present, loving the person.

If love is the answer,
Can you please repeat the question?
Once a great hero said,
"It was a million tiny little things,
When you added them all up,
They meant we were supposed to be
Together."(Tom Hanks)

You may have fights,
You may cry,
You may even be sleeping alone tonight,
Well this is life.
I might have my right and wrongs.

As Jessie J said, "Nobody is perfect!"
Learn from yesterday, live for today,
Hope for tomorrow!

And as I said before,
My life is a journey, so is yours.

Yasmin Allawi (15) 2012

One Day Too Late

Tick Tock hear the clock countdown,
Wish the minutes hand could be rewound.
So much to do, so much I need to say,
Will tomorrow be too late?

Feel the moment slip into the past,
Second by second,
Like golden sand in an hour glass,
Time passes by and I need to do everything
I said I will do.

So today I'm going to try a little harder,
Going to make every second
And minute last longer,
Because no-one has a million years,
I'm going to make the most of what I have.

So today I will reach out to somebody who needs me,
I'm going to make a change
And the world a better place
Because tomorrow may be one day too late.

Maisa Abed (11) 2012

Pen Friend

My TV broke,
I was so bored,
Until I picked up a pen,
The boredom vanished,
The words just flowed,
I lost TV but found a new friend.

David Larbi (12) 2010

People

Without people, God's lonely.
When God's here, we are his people.
We help each other.
We love and care about each other.
Love your neighbours
As your friends and family.
You were born awesome!

Be a Hero!

You don't have to do
What your friends tell you to do!

Sasha Vaughan (7) 2018

Should I?

Should I be a lady killer like Andre from Empire,
Stealing all the girls' hearts for my own devilish desire?
Lady killing from London to Paris,
I know THAT would please my great Aunt Clarice.

"Cassius, Cassius come yah! Mek sure yuh 'ave plenty a Girlfren'
No' one, no' two but plenty.
Me comin' bac' in de nex' life as a man
Heh! heh!"

Love 'em and leave 'em was what she advised me,
But love one and keep one, that's what it should be.

Should I be Rio Ferdinand for the England football team
Keeping it tight at the back, living the football dream?
Or basketball's new Steph Curry for Golden State,
Banking three pointers like make no mistake.

Should I live up to my namesake Muhammad Ali
And float like a butterfly, sting like a bee,
Phenomenal boxer well versed in poetry:

"I have wrestled with an alligator, I done tussled with a Whale,
I done handcuffed lightening, throwed thunder in jail.
That's bad! Only last week, I murdered a rock, injured a stone,
hospitalized a brick. I'm so mean I make medicine sick"

Should I think that I'm funny and make lots of money
As a comic telling family jokes.
I think of my aunties, uncles and grandad who enjoyed enter-
taining the folks:

"When me first come to Hinglan' me go fe buy cat food. De man in de shop him seh, me know you people and me know yuh going eat de cat food yuhself. Bring me de evidence and me wi' sell yuh de cat food. So me bring de puss and show de man and de man seh him sorry, him jus' have to be sure and den him sell me de cat food.

Next day me go fe buy darg food and de man seh me know yuh people, you going eat de darg food yuhself. Bring me evidence and mi wi' sell you de darg food. Me go home, bring de darg and de man sell me de darg food.

Next day me go back to de shop and put a bag on de counter. I seh me know you like fe have de evidence first, so here is de evidence, now. Can me buy some toilet roll?"

Should I be a comedian? Should I be a sportsman?
So should I be a lady-killer? No, I think I'll just be me.

Cassius Jackson-Callen (15) 2015

'Should I' was inspired by meeting and performing for Benjamin Zephaniah when WAPPY hosted an event with Hot Key Books and CCS Libraries Ealing in September 2014. Photo by Duane Jay 2014

Syria

I feel angry about the President,
He is killing people in Syria.
Nobody goes to school anymore,
Not even seven-year olds.

Every morning people come on the road
And sing a song to tell the President.
Guards are also killing people,
Taps do not work.

There is a boy in Syria,
His family died, and nobody has seen him in years
Because he hides from the President.
He is four years old.

People try to get the plane to England and Scotland,
It's really bad,
There is no part of Syria,
Which is safe.

Majd Mansour (7) 2012

Tell Me

If death is imminent, why should we try?
Why should we love if we know there's goodbye?

Why should we change just to fit in?
Why can't we just give in to sin?

Explain to me now the point of faith.
Explain how we feel secure but we're never safe.

Tell me how losing a loved one is for the best.
Tell me why we should have to pass God's test.

I beg you, show me the love in this place.
Show me the point when the dogs give chase.

Help me to see past confusion and pain.
Because right now, I fear it's all that will remain.

Lindsay Warner (14) 2012

The Counting Game

1

You put the fun in funeral and by fun,
I mean shackle the crew to your rollercoaster
because hey, at least then we're free to scream, right?

2

You put the laughter in slaughter and by laughter,
I mean slap the knee with uncontrollable giggles because hey,
what's not funny about holding the globe at gunpoint?

3

You putter the cult in culture and by cult,
I mean trees like stationary soldiers in crisp rows because hey,
why have them serve when we can serve them up?

4

You input the sin in business
and by sin, I mean just that
because hey, what else can you call genocide?

5

You put the lie in believe and by believe,
I mean the CEO's mansion levied with blood money
because hay, we've all gotta sleep somehow, right?

6

Oh. I guess we're still counting.
Maybe when I reach 100 it'll be enough.
Maybe then it'll be too late.

Lindsay Warner (20) 2018

Tiara and Crown

Life may be unsteady,
But you'll always get to the top of it.

There once was a father and daughter
Who thought they were larger than life
Until one day, their father lost his precious wife.

Then they climbed a bridge,
Thinking the only way was down.
But when they reached the top of it,
Daughter and daddy
Found their tiara and crown.

Effie Quansah-George (14) 2018

Too Late

Where were you when I was,
Hurting?
Bleeding?
Crying?

Where were you when I was,
Hungry?
Sick?
Dying?

Some of you listened
But you didn't care.

Some of you cared
But you didn't act.

Some of you acted
But you had no support.

By the time you all listen
It may be Too Late.

David Larbi (13) 2010

Unique Beat

Being different is unique
Don't feel scared or weak
When you're mad you'll feel the heat,
Just follow your heart beat.

Ricari Wilson (9) 2017

Why Am I So Tall?

People have to be free,
When they need to,
Whenever,
In a positive way
So, it is easy.
I need your help,
Why am I tall?

People need to be free,
When they need to,
I can make a change soon
But it is not easy.
Everyone join me.
Oh, why am I so tall?

Nyah Walcott-Quansah (7) 2017

This poem won first prize in the 5-8 years old category in the
Forever Young Bob Dylan Writing Contest, December 2017

Dickens: Hard Times

Artwork by Maisa Abed
2012

A Book

Please stop! Charles Dickens change the story!
I don't want to be tortured.
It may be true, but I can't bare it anymore.
I've lost my dreams.
I've lost everything.

I want my mother! I want my father!
I want my bed, not a leaking rumbling machine.

Oh please, Mr. Dickens,
It's time you ended this story of 'Hard Times.'
It's time you wrote something with love and peace.

Pick me out of this story and put me in another
book.

HARD TIMES ENDS NOW and that's final!
Mr. Charles Dickens write a happy story now.
I've had enough pain!

Maisa Abed (11) 2012

Chimney Sweeper

I wake up..... it is another day
I am cold and hungry
And I have no food to eat.
My clothes are dirty and damp.
It was raining last night
And I have no sheets to keep me warm.

At night, I fell asleep, cold and woke up cold.
I wished I lived in a fancy home,
But I don't. I clean the chimneys for the rich,
And all I get is free soot,
Covered in black from head to foot.

I count my pennies, but they are never enough.
I wish I was rich, so very much.
I have no food, I have no love,
I really wish I had a mum
To kiss and cuddle but I don't.
All I have is me.
I am a chimney sweeper.

Liliann Ferreira (8) 2012

Dickens

I'm tired of all this hurting and pain.
It wraps around my heart like a chain.
It's worse to pretend like it's not there.
Is there anything in this word that's fair?

Children with awful hurt in their eyes.
You can see it as hope withers and dies.
They've bones for blood and bruises for skin
That does nothing to hide the hurting within.

Why should children be abused?
Why should their talents be misused?
Childhood lost to the evils of man,
Who take advantage because they can.

It took a brave man to truly see,
All the wrong and misery.
He tried to connect the rich and the poor,
Yet all people did was ignore.

Now, after years have passed,
People are starting to see at last,
That Dickens' words were just and right,
On the past, he has finally shed some light.

Lindsay Warner (15) 2012

Hard Life!!

I used to do hard work all the time
I was shoved up people's chimneys
To clean out soot, which I hated so much.
I don't think children nowadays do chores
As much as I did.
Food is easy to come by
But I used to beg and beg
For food down the streets.
Some people I went to were really poor
And starving just like me.

Children nowadays cry
When they have chores to do,
But they should put themselves in my shoes.
I had a hard life. I never had any toys.
Nothing, Empty,
I did lots of work and didn't get much for it. Nothing!

I've always wanted love in the world,
But all I got was a smack. Nothing else.
I always did good in my life
So, all I deserve is love.

Izoje Owaka (10) 2012

Hard Times

Hard times can be
A loss of money,
Home, clothes or
Becoming a slave.

Hard times can be small,
Or very painful and sad.
I heard of a story,

Of a girl and her mother.
The girl's mother was very ill
And couldn't go to work.
Consequently, she didn't have enough money
To pay for rent.
Then the Landlord took away her home.
The girl's mother went to jail
And the girl went to a factory
To get money for medicine.

The girl had to do the sewing,
Washing, cleaning,
And hanging the washing
With all the other children.

One day, a visitor came
And suggested that the children
Have warm clothing.
The Factory Keeper said that
If they work hard enough
Then they would keep warm.
However, the visitor disagreed.

Many days later,
The visitor took the girl away
And gave the girl a sewing job.

Anyway, if you have a little hard time,
Please don't complain.
The Victorian times were worse.
We are very lucky to have
Money, warmth, a home and a job.

Maia Hicks (8) 2012

Hard Old Days

It turned into the hard-old days,
When the days were nights and the nights were nights,
When the days were dark, and money was tight

When we had to give our pay by the end of the day,
To the man of the house without missing out.

Working odd times, without a break,
Some went underground and some to factories,
With all the big long tunnels and the heavy machinery.

"Dangerous as hell letting kids near that!"
One of us said.
We heard, he never came back.

Another day has just gone passed,
Lying in bed,
Thinking to myself about the hard-old days and how it went,
With the pressure in my head just for a piece of bread.

Look at today,
What don't we have?
For everything in life, we take the easy way,
And if worse comes to worst we can choose to face the
opportunities,
We didn't take, so come on say, "yes!"

Hard Times!

Sonam Ubhi (15) 2012

Hard Work, Hard Times!

In the olden days
Children experienced hard times.
They had to clean the roads
Because it got messy every day.
They worked and worked and worked
Until they collapsed.

No air in the mines,
Just dusty, smelly conditions
And long hours.
If a child was poor,
You had a bad education, or no education
Children did not have a choice
To do what they wanted.
Some even had to sweep chimneys
Oh ...what hard times!

Nowadays, most children have a choice
About what they want to do.
Because now there are laws,
And no one wants to break them...
Or do they???
Sadly, hard times still exist
For children all over the world,
Because some countries are still poor
And can't pay their debts.

There are children,
Who are treated like slaves,
Some children are fighting for their countries.

Should they have to do that?
I say, "no!"
What do you say?
Well...we should be grateful for what we have got
Huh...what a life of hard times!

Effie Quansah-George (9) 2012

It Can Be Hard Being Short

Hard times, hard times.
Why is it always me?
Is it because I'm short?
Is it because I'm poor?
Why is it always me?

Hard times, hard times.
You laugh and laugh.
Is it really funny?

Hard times, hard times.
Put yourself in my shoes.
Carry on laughing but I won't care.
I'd rather die than stay alive.
All because of you!

Hard times, hard times
Why is it always me?
I'm not going to let you in!
I'm going to fight and fight until you lose!
Hard times, hard times

Reem Omar (10) 2012

My Depressing Life!!!

I wake up to another depressing day,
Always the same, never something new!
Ready to play my game,
Crawling behind the thick furry coats,
Taking all the money,
My little hands can carry,
Stealing fresh green apples and delicious food,
Laying the little money I have on the broken and tatty table.

It's cold and my clothes are wet, ripped and tatty,
No fire to keep me warm,
And a house to keep me from all the bad things.
I have no clothes to keep me warm in the winter,
No shoes to keep my feet dry and warm from the puddles,
Oh, how I wish to have all these things!

Emilia Ferreira (12) 2012

My Hard Times

It was very hard back in the olden days.
I was made to work gruelling hours,
And at the end of the day,
Only got paid a few pennies.
Hardly enough for food or clothes.

I would work as hard as I possibly could.
My Master could whip me any time he liked.
Over the past few days
I've been planning to run away to the countryside.

Since I was thrown out of the small room
That I used to live in,
Until my mother died, and my father left me,
I have been moving to different locations.
Approximately fifteen times now!

If you hate your life now,
And have read this, then change.
Change now!!

Ida Mwangi (10) 2012

My Life

I'm 18 ... so what?
I'm doing this for my country and this is what I get?
I'm a black 18-year-old footballer.
You people go off and change the rules,
Spoil my life and all that I was waiting for.
Is it because I am black,
Or because I'm from a different culture?

It's time you stop and think about the world!
I am human.
You are human.
We both have human rights.
It's time you realise we're all equal.
It's time to live together.

No hard times.
Just love in our dreams.

Yasmin Allawi (15) 2012

Recycled Information

Today is brand new,
No old factories or telephones,
Just brand-new cars and brand new homes.
Whenever we need money we take a loan.
Whenever we're disliked we're left alone.
Whenever the dogs are hungry you give her a bone,
When our kids need to learn you teach them what you know.
So they teach others what they've been shown.

If you didn't notice,
Brand new is only a nicer replication of the old.
If you did notice,
Good observation,
Taught down the blood line.

Recycled information,
Yet still in good condition,
No searching up the definition,
Just using your intuition.
The past is the demolition of the present,
And the future is the reconstruction of the past.
Our ancient role models brought upon the modern age,
All throughout the nation, taught down the blood line.
Recycled information.
Never mind what we're inventing,
Now, look what we've invented,
Already, from cavemen's wheels to meals on wheels,
From flints and stones to mobile phones,
From Victorian gruel to public school,
From rats and bats to aristocrats.

Before you think about publication,
Remember!
Taught down the blood line...
Recycled information!!

Benjamin Eshun (14) 2012

feelings

Artwork by Fransica Simmonds
2016

About the Love

I am me,
You are you,
I'm fantastic
And you are too!

I love me
You love you
And we should learn
To love each other too.

Yeah, I said
We should learn to
Love each other too!

Isla Heath (9) 2014

Fear

Fear lives inside everyone
No matter who you are
Or where you're from
It lurks deep down
Waiting for the right moment
Like a tiger waiting to pounce on its prey
And when the time comes
Fear will take over
Eliminating all other emotions
Leaving you at its mercy
There's nowhere you can hide
As fear is a part of you
And once its job is done
It returns to its lair deep down
Never resting
Only waiting
Until the right moment...

Nathan Warner (13) 2008

If I Take You

If I take you to space my love we will be infinity,
And beyond like a rocket ship.
Even NASA had to give us a first-class flight.
I must be thinking of our love at first sight
And not even giving up on our fight
Because my lips stay tight,
Only for you my love.

If I can be your knight in shining armour,
It will be our own honour, as we ride off into the night,
As twilights,
I had to write about them until daylight,
On the seen sight,
Because your eyes are also my headlights,
Within my direction into the moonlight.

If tonight we will unite
As I give you a love bite,
Means I have to be polite
For you are my crown heights.
I know I overwrite love.

But it's how I experience you from first sight
I want to make you and I our own ray of light,
Strong like iron,
But I do know it sounds ironic but it's symbolic
Because love is my goal.
Why can't it be real?
So, let's follow our own hearts.
Here is where my heart and yours will be.

Great and we'll do our part,
Like from the start,

As you are my forever Queen of Hearts
And I'm your King of Hearts.
I don't want to break hearts nor depart.

Kieran Ross (2018)

Love

Love is magic
Magic with a meaning
Meanings full of hope
Hope that is reliable.
Reliable when your life turns upside
Down till you think
You can't get it up any more
More for you
I'm hidden in our corner waiting
To be found.

Renée Dawkins (10) 2013

Love?

What is love? I really don't know.
Is love a feeling or a thing?
Is love really meaningful
Or is it just a fling?

What is love? I really don't know.
Does it make you feel butterflies everywhere?
Or is it just a feeling
That makes you want to fix your hair?

What is love?
I don't know what it will be.
All I know is that
I'll have to wait and see!

Eleanor Howard (12) 2018

My Voice Echoes

I sit quietly while the music plays,
My mum enters the room, smiling,
Telling me she heard me singing earlier,
I smile back and look for the song she likes.

It's quiet for a moment.
We are both standing,
Waiting for the silence to be filled,
However, it doesn't work,
The music doesn't play.

Mum looks at me,
So I do something else,
I close my eyes and sing.
My voice echoes around the room.
It bounces off the walls,
At this point mum leaves.

I sit back down thinking,
Maybe it's the song,
What if Mum doesn't like it?
As I'm about to turn the music on,
Mum comes back,
She's holding something in her hand.
I look once and then again,
A microphone!
"Keep singing Princess," she said.

Sarai Aidoo-Richardson (14) 2018

Passion

Passion can make you sing and cry
Love or lie.
It can be daily,
For a lucky person.
It can come one in a million,
In a different version.

It's deeper than the seas
That rage above the trees.
Its feeling is speechless
And true in faithfulness.

Niyil Gayle-Jackson (11) 2008

Share My Love

Someone, please rescue me!
For I'm sure I can take no more,
Your beauty tortures me every day,
Its unattainability taunts me from a distance away.

'Tis only fair that I gain respite,
For your ravishing looks burn my eyes,
Your voice like honey, your hair like silk,
Your skin unblemished your eyes have built.

A thirst unquenchable 'till here,
Your hand I have and if it costs me dear,
What do I care?
Because to me,
You are the only thing I'll ever need.

You have lured me in, I'm in your snare.
I'll never leave you and will always be there
And my love for you we'll finally share.

David Larbi (13) 2011

To Linda

I love you because
You are the best
In the world
And when you need help
I will come to you.

When you see
All the ice cream
You will love the colours
And the sparkles
But you need pennies
To buy the ice-cream
With the sparkles.

Athena Ioannou (8) 2018

Yellow

Yellow is a bright colour that symbolises happiness,
The colour of the sun, honey and syrup;
A colour that lifts your spirits and takes away sadness,
When I look at its beauty, it makes me cheer up.

Thinking of sunshine makes me smile,
A pop of colour in the never-ending blue sky,
I love to laugh and laugh for a while,
And this will never change,
For in my heart I have a little light of mine.

Sarah Larbi (11) 2018

Young Love

I love her to bits and pieces
If she cries, I cry too.
If she smiles, I smile,
If she's this, I'm that.

I would love to be her shadow,
So that I can be with her forever.
She's my life, my world, my everything
And she is in my dreams.

I love her too much
Though, I'm shy to talk to her
But there will be one day
When I will let it all out...

"I love her!"

Reem Omar (13) 2014

Girls Shout Out

Artwork by Fransica Simmonds
2016

Different Me!

I acted like a kid
I lost everything;
Popularity
Friendship
Love
Respect

I pushed away the people,
Who I loved the most
And the people who wanted me to change.
I had to change,
I seriously know that now.
But how?

Now I sit in the corner having flashbacks,
On the mistakes I have made
Over and over again.

I wanted to change.
I do! I do! I do!
But how?

I am not changing because of people.
I am changing because it's started to
Affect me and my school work.

I needed to.
I have to become a different me.

Izoje Owaka (13) 2015

Goodbye Walking, Hello Crutches

On a regular day,
On a regular afternoon,
My Mum kept nagging, nagging
And nagging again,

"Take your plate to the kitchen,
Help your Nana Out!"
I said "I willllllll if you don't shout!"
Whilst taking my plate

I trip, stumble and fall
The table leg separates my toes...
That is so uncool!

Day 3. Walking into the hospital,
All brave and fingers crossed.
So, taking the plate
Made me pay the cost.

The X-ray showed my toes were broken
Suddenly my mum's eyes had woken
"Effie...what have you done?
Now walking isn't so fun!"

Hopping out of the helpful Hammersmith Hospital,
With crutches and a cast
Now I am so hungry,
Don't think I'm going to last.

Two hours later,
I'm finally in my bed
All the memories of today's events
Are swimming in my head!

Effie Quansah-George (11) 2015

I Asked My Mum, the Answer is "NO!"

"When I grow up, can I become a mountain?"
"No!"

"When I grow up can I become a football?"
"No!"

"When I grow up can I become a TV?"
"No!"

"When I grow up can I become a tree?"
"No!"

'When I grow up can I become a sofa?"
"No!"

"When I grow up can I become a book?"
"No!"

"When I grow up can I become a ..."
"No! No! No! No! Nooooooooo!"

"Well then, what can I become when I grow up?"
"You can be a grown up."

"Well, that's boring!
Then I never want to grow up!"

Gerda Kleinberga (10) 2015

Legendary Women Rule the World

Women we are powerful
Women we are strong
We are all independent
This is where we belong

Women we are courageous
We can win the battle
We are all modest
We are very practical

Women we are mature
It is the best way we can be
We all love a good laugh
This is the best way to be free

We are legends
We can rule the world some day
That is why we are celebrating women today.

Jessica. M. Howard (11) 2015

Women and Men

Men go to war, so do women,
Men can drive cars, so can women,
Men can be butchers, so can women,
Well now anyway.

Men are allowed to be painters, so are women,
Men give birth, so do women...

Wait.... let me think about that one...
ONLY women can give birth,
And they give birth to both men and women.
So be thankful to women all you guys!!
'Cause if there were no women, there would be no you!

Gerda Kleinberga (11) 2015

WAPPY Members receive awards after performance at Ealing Women's Forum Awards from Dr. Rupa Huq MP. (Ealing Central and Acton) and Jacky Sear. Rick Yard, June 2015, Walpole Park, West London

Going for Gold

Artwork by Acquaye McCalman

An Acrostic Poem

Oh, what joy, the time has come
London Olympics has begun
Years have waited for our athletes
Millions come to see their countries compete
People's emotional stories warm hearts
In the great anticipation of the start
Choose from long distance, running and show jumping tricks
So, let's join as one for these Olympics

Paul Larbi (10) 2012

Be the Best

Run hard, run soft
Only think of two things
The gun and the tape.
When you hear one just run like,
Hell, until you break the other.
Have the determination to run.
Have the aggression of your race.
Get the crowd moving
Be quicker than the gun.
But run, run like Harold Abrahams
and Usain Bolt!

Emelia Ferreira (11) 2012

Football

You don't have to be tall,
To play football,
But Arsenal are
The Superstars!

I am the striker,
And no one else is
Except for me,
My team are 3rd in the league

Robin Van Persie
And Macheda,
They are two of the best,
And have lots of zest

Red is my favourite colour
That is why
I like Arsenal,
They are wonderful!

Sami Baramo (7) 2012

Football is Everything

Football is everything.
Over excited and feeling nervous before the match.
Observing the other team,
To predict how well they'll play.
Best bit is when I score,
And the crowd starts chanting my name.
Learning how to be part of a team.
Loving every second of the game.

Jack Joshua (8) 2018

It's All About Football

I do training first,
Yesterday I did a shot
Then I scored!
And everyone said, "goal!"
The team said, "goal,"
And daddy said, "good."

When I was tackling
I just did a shot,
Then I scored!
I want to be a footballer.

Messi is very good,
At skills,
He plays for Argentina.
I play with Arsenal,
And their uniform is red.

There's Aubameyang,
He plays for Arsenal,
There's also Ozil
They lost last week,
But they won yesterday.

I wake up early
To go to football.
Yesterday I was,
Man of the Match
Because I scored.

Arsène Wenger wasn't playing
That much good
I want to be a footballer
Not a manager

I play at the front of the goal.
There is a boy
Who doesn't pass
The ball to his team

When we score
We do a celebration.
When I score
Daddy says, "Well done Quincey."

Quincey Walcott-Quansah (4) 2018

No-one Can Outrun Bolt

What?
Bolt beaten, defeat-en ...
By this ... Yohan Blake
Twice ...
That isn't nice ...

But wait!
Bolt strikes back
And wins back his glory.
His defeats in the trials were
Only temporary ...
His performance varies ...
Not in the best of shape
At that time.
But Bolt knew he would be fine.

This was just a warm up for him
And his rival/friend.
He was well aware
He'd be running again.
He knew he would win
And he did.
Outrunning all other men,

For in the trials
There was only a little fault with Usain Bolt.

Ben Eshun (14) 2012

Olympia

Olympia was such a poor place but think again!
That was where the Olympics first took place.
There was Javelin, running, and all sorts of sports.
Now, let's get on to the Olympic torch! It shines so bright.
People run with it and pass it on.
Certain people get to hold the Olympic torch.
The Olympic Rings have these five colours: blue, yellow, green,
red and black.
That is because you will find one in each one of the countries
flags.

Mary Mikhaeil (6) 2012

Super Pole

The Olympic stadium
Is where all the countries
Come to see their athletes,
Women run with a pole,
Jump over a High bar,
And land on a BIG crash-mat.
I like this jump because you have to
Push yourself so High.

Kaiaanu Shepnekhi-Boston (7) 2012

The Back Flip

I like jumping and spinning around
I like the back-flips and tumbling
Do you know what it is called?
JIM-NAS-TICKS

Mesentis Shepnekhi-Boston (4) 2012

The Olympics

A time for coming together.
A time when critics are proved wrong.
A time when years of hard work will yield rich rewards.
A time when people of all nations rise as one.
A time of new beginnings.
A time for fulfilling dreams.
A time for achieving greatness.
A time for overcoming challenge.
A time for inspiration.
Not just a time.
Our time.

Daniel Larbi (12) 2012

The Olympics

The Olympics
First held in Greece,
Women were not aloud
To watch or run
Unless they were not married!

Grace Simons (7) 2012

135

Train Hard!

At the end of the Olympics
We all say sorry if we lose
And shout out, "yeah!" if we win....
Competitive or not competitive,
Please be good and if not just say,
"At the end of the day,"
You represented your country.
Don't be a sour loser
Be a nice watermelon.

Usain Bolt lost twice,
Came back in four years,
And came 1st and beat his own score,
Like China, it has been really good,
Great Britain has done really good,
Though not good enough!

At the end of the Olympics,
We all say we did do good.
But next time we will do better;
It's not the end of the world.
So, don't be mad because you just took part
And somebody may pick on you,
Because they came first, and you came last
Rather, say "bog off!" ....
'Cause next year you will do better
Than they did next time,

Usain Bolt got defeated twice
But he trained harder, returned,
And returned and beat his enemy.

Don't worry because everybody has different skills,
BOLT is running, China.. Gymnastics.
GB ...tennis, and many other skills
So if you want to be in the Olympics,
Train hard.

Izoje Owaka (10) 2012

People Who Have Changed the World

BENJAMIN ZEPHANIAH

Benjamin Zephaniah Meets WAPPY, Ealing Central Library, 2014

Benjamin Zephaniah

Oh Benjamin Zephaniah!
Whoever you are!
Are you a star?
But wait.... are you the one
Who was fun,
When you performed 'Talking Turkeys'?
Yes! It's coming back to me!
I live your poetry!

Effie Quansah-George (7) 2011

The People's Poetical Friend

Brother Benjamin Zephaniah,
Your poetry and lyrics keep us ever-inspired.
Grounded reasonings are rife
Of your political passions in life.

With humour and honesty, you connect with your fans,
By keeping it real and making a stand,
On grassroots issues including animal rights,
Through your work, young and mature aspire to great heights.

On 15th April 2018, 60 Earthstrong years you celebrate!
I wish you eternal happiness on this special date,
Congratulations on your new book, an exciting biography,
As soon as I can I'll buy one to read.

Give thanks Brother Ben,
For supporting our local libraries' campaign,
And for biggin up WAPPY,
You've inspired members to immeasurable ends.
In Jah's time I'm sure Ealing will welcome you again,

Bless up, Happy Earth Day, Peace and Love
The people's poetical friend.

Akuba 2018

Internationally acclaimed Dub Poet, Musician & Writer, Professor Benjamin Zephaniah with WAPPY Team Members, Akuba, John Durston, Rahwa Ghergish, Ben Pozi-Quansah & Ealing Library's Manager, WAPPY, 2014. Photo by Duane Jay

People Who Have Changed the World
BOB DYLAN

Artwork by Kai Sim
2017

Bob Dylan

Being a different religion isn't being wrong,
Only people who have a heart stay true to their family,
Be supportive of my instrument choices and what I play,

Don't be the one to take my picture,
You must not judge who has succeeded and is happy,
Love your family you never know when you will lose them,
All my Grammy's and you neglect my song choice,
New York is the city that launched my career.

Seren Sim (11) 2017

Bob Dylan, the Man

Bob Dylan the man, how you took the world by fame!
Occupying his fans, he stood there on the stage,
Bluesing and cruising with the fans booing and 'oohing'.

Driving the fans up and down,
Yawn, yawn, yawn until dawn,
Laying his head in his hands he hit the pain,
A song that drove his fame under,
Never have I've seen such as fame drop!

T-Khai James-Palmer-Wahome-Kellehey (9) 2017

Dear Mr Dylan

As a boy you were motivated,
By the most influential in the world,
You sat at your turntable and admired your vinyl.
Elvis, Jerry Lee, Little Richard,
The man you used to imitate at high school dances.
Fizzy notes and charming voices.

You didn't know this young, Mr Dylan,
But you were already true to the phrases,
You would soon swear by;
"You better start swimming or you'll sink like a rock".

And suddenly the years went by and you were a man.
A young one though, and oh how you swam!
Your fingers on the guitar,
Your songs keeping us calm.

Oh, bright star on that wondrous stage!
And, Mr Dylan, "how times they are a-changing",
You're 76 now and oh...
"I'm glad to see you alive, you're looking like a saint."

Renée Dawkins (15) 2017

Listen to My Song

When I was young I stamped my foot
So, everyone listened to my song.
My family, especially, my grandma.

Then I started playing the harmonica
And guitar and made a band with my friends.
I started with Rock and Roll,
Then Country, then Gospel,
Which won me many friends.

I got to see Martin Luther King
And felt pleased with myself.

Aniya Thompson (8) 2017

Prize Peace

I ran to the highest tree to see peace,
In the heat.
I sang, 'Holy to the World of Peace',
My fans were screaming,
Which made me proud.
I won the Nobel Prize and Grammy award.

Dewaine Thompson (10) 2017

Songs Inspire Many

One man, many wonders,
His life, His story,
His poems, His songs,
Forever in my memory

'I shall be Released'
A song about a trapped soul,
Awaiting to be set free,
To come out of society's control

'Blowing in the Wind'
A song about the hopes we could possess,
But we can't see it right in front of us,
Since at this moment, we live in darkness

'To make You Feel My Love'
A song about how we should support each other,
In our weaknesses and struggles,
Instead of destroying one another.

His songs inspire many,
To become better people
To give hope to others,
To be a light on a hill.

Ivy Oppong (14) 2017
Contest Winner

The Passionate Poet

Bob Dylan, Bob Dylan,
He was the one who in 1963
Performed at the Civil Rights March,
In Washington, where Martin Luther King,
Presented his favourite speech, 'I have a dream'.

He is an artist, an inspirational person
Who changed music,
And pushed limits to the furthest,
With his love of Gospel songs, Country,
Blues and Black Rhythm records.
The same boy who played with chalk boards.
In 1966, Bob thought his life was coming to an end quickly,
But luckily, he made his recovery rather swiftly.

Dylan writes his music with lots of passion,
Even though he has atrocious fashion!
I still love Bob Dylan, Bob Dylan.

Awards and prizes lead to great success
One album by him, 'Time Out of Mind', was his best,
Overall, Bob Dylan is a singer, performer,
An idol to all who was neglected by a crowd,
For not singing their choice of music,
They spoke quite clear and loud.
But Bob Dylan listened and sang with passion,
To the people, he sang out proud.

Before I was at a loss to,
Why you are a star,
And what you do....
Now I know you wrote the best tunes
Bob Dylan, Bob Dylan,
I love your music too!

Effie Quansah-George (14) 2017

Artwork by Leilani Drummey
2017

To Love or To Lose

To love or to lose,
A familiar choice that we have all been through.
Things that we love can slip away from our grasp,
But when we forget the small, fabulous things,
Everything can come crashing down.

A smile is an uncontrollably contagious force:
Happiness,
A force like love that can bend sad emotions,
And build friendship towers that can go higher and higher,
When people break this happiness disaster can spread,

These towers fall, towers of trust and friendship,
Times of sadness, times of need,
These people come in handy but not if we abuse them,
Then we lose, then we lose them.

Think about this poem and any time you've abused,
Now go say, "sorry!"
Spread happiness, and remember,
Love or lose.

Mark Mwangi (10) 2017
Contest Winner

Unique Beat

Being different is unique
Don't feel scared or weak
When you're mad you'll feel the heat,
Just follow your heart beat.

Ricari Wilson (9) 2017

People Who Have Changed the World

BOB MARLEY

Artwork by Ivy Oppong
2015

A Legacy That Is Priceless

We had Memorial Day,
To honour the military
Who murder for money,
But nothing for this visionary.
It's killing me, the thought of humanity in such misery,
And Bob Marley shared the same views.
He had love for the truth,
Put his love in the music
Spread his essence into progeny till he was murdered by his
 enemies.

No, wait...!
That's a "conspiracy theory!"
If I include those, the doubters won't be hearing me clearly
Lemme end like this, although he's lifeless,
His likeness lives on in a legacy that is priceless
To Bob Marley.

Michael Larbi (17) 2015

A Message for You

Bob Marley, oh Bob Marley
What a legend
What a Rasta
What a successful person
What a talented man

Bob Marley, oh bob Marley
What a singer!
What a performer!
Bob Marley, oh Bob Marley
How was it like to have long hair?
What was it like to create songs,
Which have a big impact on people?
What was it like to have dreadlocks?
Did you like people calling you a Rasta?

Bob Marley, oh Bob Marley
I love your songs especially
Three Little Birds,
Because that song has a message
FOR YOU OO OO

Izoje Owaka (13) 2015

Bob Marley

Bright like the sun shining throughout the day
Observant like the owl awake at night
Believer, he follows not the good, not
    the bad but pursues God

Making peace like two enemies shaking hands
Amazing like a breath-taking moment
Rastafarian was his faith that he embraced
Legendary like no other artist
Exceptional for protesting for rights and beliefs
Young Palm reader from the age of five
    but sadly, too young to die

Effie Quansah-George (11) 2015

Bob Marley

Bullied, teased, named,
Is this what life is meant to be?
Bob Marley believed it was wrong,
Do you agree?

He fought for peace, he fought for hope
So, the future life could cope,
A person who was once told,
'Don't gain the world and lose your soul,
Wisdom is better than silver or gold'
Many will agree like you and me.

Bob Marley remains in our hearts
Now and until we part.

Bob Marley, RIP.
Peace is with you.

Ivy Oppong (11) 2015

Bob Marley

Bob lived in a slum
And now see what he has become.
He was on God's side,
He got bullied because of that,
But he did not hide under a mat.

He showed them what he was made of,
His neighbour called him, 'White Boy',
Bob was not white or black.
He was mixed,
And he was proud of that.

Then he wanted to make peace,
Make the world good.
He is an influence on us,
To write songs and make the world a better place.
Make bad good and good excellent.
We follow him in his lyrics,
Such as 'One Love' and,
'No Woman No Cry'.

Kyra Nelson (8) 2015

Bob Marley

Strong, Powerful,
Successful Singer,
As an Individual,
We are Strong,
Peace Unites Us,
Together as One

Leilani Drummey (11) 2015

Bob Marley?

Bob Marley... who?
Nesta they say
The light black boy
Living with Rita
Having fun in Kingston

Number four was his age
When he read palms,
Getting people's lives right
Quite cool, right?

But then he got the feeling of the beat
He left those palms for the heat
To be a musician,
Why was that?
Yes, it was why, exactly why

So, there he is smoking spliff
What a life!
Drinking that rum, how nice,
Take it slow,
That's what he did,
Listening to music,
Where did it go?

He was strong,
Cancer didn't take him down.
It took him up,
Built some strength

He's dead now
Death had to choose
And it chose him

Renée Dawkins (13) 2015
Poetry Contest Winner

Bob Marley and Me

Bob Marley and me - we have a history.
When Bob Marley was born,
I was frogspawn,
A mere twinkle in my father's eye.
When Bob Marley died, and the world cried
I was still 17 years in the making.

As a Primary School boy with my Tamagotchi toy
A bully waylaid me one day.
He was the big tree, I was the small axe
I cut him down - those are the facts.

My grandma Milly, a Jamaican Hillbilly
loved Bob's lyrics and tunes
"Dat deh buoy ca' sing, a pur jiy him bring
Feget yuh trouble an' dance."

Beefy Jo, "him nyam an' go"
Belly full but him hungry still.
He collapsed on my leg, like a full beer keg
And shattered my ankle in pieces.

Plaster cast to my knee. Oh Lord, why me?
I was a boy who loved sporting and ramping
So I waited in vain to Lively Up myself again
As I listened to Bob's rebel music.

Exodus was pretty cool from Junior to High School
As I worked to be popular an' all that.

I jammed with three little birds and laughed at the nerds
As I enjoyed my beef with my teachers.

No woman no cry as I watched my grades die
And Mum was on my case
"Open your eye and look within.
Are you satisfied with the life you're living?"

So, Bob's lyrics lifted my spirits.
He taught me to emancipate myself from mental slavery
as none but ourselves can free our minds.

He taught me living for myself is living in vain.
He taught me how in this great future,
We can't forget the past.

So, Bob Marley and me - we have a history.

Cassius Jackson-Callen (15) 2015

Bob Marley, I will Miss You

Bob Marley, I will miss you,
And all the inspirational things you do;
Your songs make me free,
Your words make me realise the real me.

Bob Marley, I will miss you
And all the inspirational things you do;
You make the world see things in a different way,
You make sad children want to laugh and play.

Bob Marley, I will miss you
And all the inspirational things you do;
I will remember you for your songs and wisdom,
You have taken me out of my imaginary prison;
Bob Marley,
I will miss you.

Jessica M Howard (11) 2015

Inspired by listening to "Don't Worry, Be Happy". Poetry Contest Winner.

Bob Rasta Marley

ONE LOVE
JAMAICA

Jack Joshua (5) 2015

I Am Nesta Robert Marley

I was younger
I was older
I was white
I was black
I was sad
I was happy
I was Nesta Robert Marley

I am the mathematics genius
I am the true palm reader
I never had such a brain
To think that people can hurt you with such small words,
Stunning people with such irritating personalities
That can give you the guts to say what you think about them

I loved all kinds of ladies and especially the ones with babies
The ones who have such beautiful personalities and looks

I am Nesta Robert Marley
I was the one who was motivated,
Motivated by the prisoners, would be shocking for some people
This was until metal flew into my eye and my vision changed
I still loved the ladies, especially the ones with babies
I never had much talent,
Only smoking really with the ladies the most
Until people began to queue up for me to read their palms,
Until I found the one, the only one I can think of now.
I started to refuse to read more palms,
And that was the end of my talent

I proposed to her,
I thought it was too quick, but I did it
And it was a "yes"!
Her name was Rita,
Rita Anderson
I was playing football, trying to impress her,
As I always do

I don't know what happened
But I felt like I didn't have any feet
Or anything in mind really
It was only a small injury I guess,
I left it for a while 'till I thought it got too serious,
I started limping to the doctors,
They said I had to cut off my foot,
But I refused!
I told them,
I am a Rastafarian,
I am born to be natural
And become how I was created by God

My cancer got even worse,
It started getting into my heart
I had trouble breathing
I am Nesta Robert Marley

Thank you for everything God

Sara Abed (13) 2015

I Really Don't Know How I Got Started

As we unearth the ground
We find our roots
Where it all started fear drives me,
But as you unearth me
You do not find anything

I knew I wanted it
I never really had to start
I never let fear drive me
My ambition led me
On the way I lost good friends

I was illustrated on the wall
I got 'Song of the Millennium'
I shared the love
I shared 'One Love'
Yet I still don't know where it started...

Maisa Abed (14) 2015

Make Peace

People have said such horrible things,
But on the other side,
"Everything will be alright."

Remember that hope is still,
In your heart,
Even if you've lost someone special,
Or someone has made you upset
Peace will make everyone united.

Make Peace.

Imara Turney (11) 12015

Marley's Whisper

I walked outside my mansion
And outside I saw these random
Three little birds with such fashion
That gave my mind an expansion

At first, I was such a nutter
Who got into many tantrums
Had dreadlocks but was no Rasta
And now I will tell you mandem

Good things come to those who listen
There's no need for competition
No pain and no ammunition
What I speak are words of wisdom

If you take offence, I'm sorry
I just don't want people to fight
A wise man once said "don't worry..."
"Cause everything will be alright"

And reggae is underrated
Some people say it's outdated
They just care about pop music
Which is why they're all deluded

We should all listen to Marley
Cause I know he's right up above
Whispering to us all calmly
"There's One Life,
One Heart, and One Love."

Acquaye McCalman (20) 2015

One Love

Will Keep
The Peace
It doesn't matter,
What faith we are,
We are all one and,
God will love us
For that!

It doesn't matter
What faith we are,
We shall love each other
And live and love in the
Example of the Almighty

I'm your father,
Your mother,
I'm your bredrin,
Your sistren,
Together one love
Will keep the peace.

Nazir Gentry (10) 2015

Peace On Earth

I dream of a land where there is no war or conflict
A place of peace and happiness
Where the sky is always clear of troubles
And every day the sun shines on us

The dogs do not bite or bark at us
And the bees never sting
Everyone is fit and healthy
And can never get sick or injured

Every family will never get separated
And has no members missing
They all have a room each
With enough food for months
Everyone goes to work and gets money
And their children go to school everyday

There is no discrimination of any kind
No one is a slave, and everyone is free
Everyone has a voice and all their rights
Everyone is always speaking freely

If we are one with God
This dreamland will become a reality

Maia Hicks (11) 2015

RIP

If life had more people like Bob,
Less people would start to sob.
His personality was right,
His music was always bright.
RIP Bob Marley
We will keep you in our hearts.

Tamzin Chapman (11) 2015

The Life of Bob

When Bob was young,
He lived in a slum,
People bullied him,
Because of his race.
They bullied him, Saying,
"You no black or white"
Bob fought for things that were right

Some people are mindlessly dumb
Bob did things the way they should be done
We need more people like Bob
He was a man of faith in God.

Lola Joshua (8) 2015
Poetry Contest Winner

The Man Who Feels the Rain

Bob was bullied,
And called a 'White boy'
But he said,
He was not on the 'White side'
And not on the Black side.
He's on 'God's side.'

He was four years old
When he noticed
He could read palms,
He was truly gifted,
I'm inspired by Bob's quote:
"Some people feel the rain,
Others just get wet."

Christopher Ioannou (11) 2015

We Will Remember Him

His father was white
His mother was black
He lived to fight
To make a pack
Of people who promoted peace
And so we will remember him

At the age of four
He could see the future
But he was desperately poor
Even though he has a lot of humour
And so we will remember him

He was infected by cancer
But he didn't lose the limb
And all of his banter
Was not at all dim
And so we will remember him

He died in 1981
And we will remember him
His time was lots of fun
And so, we will remember him

Ida Mwangi (13) 2015

What Bob Marley is Like

Bob Marley played loud music
He is a very kind person
He is a very famous person
He is a very interesting person
He is a very funny man

Maisha Thomas (6) 2015

When Bob Marley Was a Child

When Bob Marley was a child,
He was bullied,
Because he was mixed race,
People were saying
"You're not from Jamaica,
You're white boy!"
They said,
"You don't belong in Jamaica."

Chad Turney (8) 2015

People Who Have Changed the World
MARCUS GARVEY

Drawing by Alydia R. Thompson

Marcus Garvey

Living in a world of chaos
Standing for rights
Relying on yourself
The world depends on you

Marcus Garvey, Black Star
Always doing best
Reading dictionaries
With his best friends

Joyce was sent to England
To never speak a word
Surrenders very quietly
Marcus Garvey

Marcus Garvey, Black Star
Always doing best
Reading dictionaries
With his best friends

An inspiration to all,
A leader of black rights,
Influence to black people
Marcus Garvey

A Song by Eleanor Howard (9)
and Seren Sim (9) 2016

My One and Only Dream

I am sailing in my ship
But no ordinary one.
A ship that will take me
To the Seven Seas.
The seas that I have been
Wishing to go to.

It is wet, cold and misty.
And sharks dive up.
Will I ever be able to get there?
"No", I thought!
I will keep going on.
When I look up
I see something glowing.
Can it be treasure?

I sail as fast as I can
And there it was!
After thirty-five years
It has finally come true,
My one and only dream!

Aaliyah Momoh (8) 2018

What Was in the Trunk?

When the Trunk was opened
Lots of special,
Different things were found,
For example, the Captain's hat,
An old box full of old money,
Family photos and a sketch
Of Marcus Garvey,
The Captain,
Kwame Nkrumah and
The Empire State Building

Kiki Thompson (11) 2017

People Who Have Changed the World
JESSICA HUNTLEY

An Honest Tribute

Honestly, I don't know what to talk about.
Maybe I'll start with talking about the long struggle for black people,

Settling into western countries such as our own England.
At first, they were treated like a different species,
People were surprised to see a 'new' kind of people with darker skin,
And springy hair.

Some people were accepting of these people,
Others weren't too keen on the idea of a 'new kind of human'.

Those who opposed them had tried everything in their power to strike us down,
But it was thanks to people like Jessica Huntley that we stood our ground,
And fought back successfully.

Jessica Huntley was a Guyanese-born black publisher,
A campaigner for civil rights,
Who also helped to inspire young people to read and write,
Even though she was older and wiser than most of her peers,
She could still relate to people of all years.

To be honest, I spent about two weeks
Wondering what to write for today.
I had no idea what to talk about.
I knew who Jessica Huntley was,
but I didn't know her well enough to write a poem about her.

I was just told by a numerous number of names
That she had played an important role in our community.
I was aware of this, but I didn't really think much of it

Until I found out she had passed away.
That is when I realised how important of a person she was.

She had even published my first poems a few years back.
I now feel honoured to know that they were published by Bogle
L'Ouverture Press,
They really must have been impressed with my work.

Mother Huntley was a positive black figure
And role model to many younger generations.
She helped to promote black literature to our community
And our literature to all communities.

Even though it is sad to have lost an inspirational figure,
Mother Huntley has left a positive impact on young people,
Older people and whole communities,
Which will continue to resonate for years to come.

Ben Eshun (15) 2014

*Benjamin read this poem in memory of Jessica Huntley at the 9th Huntley
Archives Conference, London Metropolitan Archives (LMA), 2014.*

People Who Have Changed the World
MICHAEL JACKSON

Painting by Yan Pei-Ming
in memory of Michael Jackson, 2017

Michael Jackson

From Africa to concerts,
And gloves to dinner jackets,
From music to heart throbs,
And friends to superfans,
From songs to inpiration
And Michael Jackson.

Ivy Oppong (14) 2018

Michael Jackson

One day he's here
The next he is gone.
He came to rock my world
But he is gone too soon.
He is the world
And we are the children.
He is safe at rest
The problems are over.
We know that we are not alone
That you are here with us.
May your soul
Rest in peace.

Henrietta Perry (12) 2009

People Who Have Changed the World
WILLIS WILKIE

Belated Goodbye

As we lay your body in the grave,
Your spirit's strolling through the gates.
You can walk up to God
And say your life was not a waste.
Mr Wilkie - father,
Pastor and teacher,
Brother in Christ,
Strong community leader.
Our heads are bowed
But you can hold yours high
With pride. Goodbye.
See you on the other side.

Michael Larbi (17) 2013

Perfect Peace

In a small minute,
You were snatched away by the cold hands of death.
You lived a very inspirational life,
And I am thankful I got to meet you
and be a part of Your life for a short while.
May your soul rest in perfect peace,
Mr Wilkie.

Henrietta Perry (16) 2013
Henrietta interviewed Mr. Wilkie with her sister, Catherine Perry [12], for the Root to The Fruit Heritage Lottery- funded Oral History Project, August 2011.

A Simple Yet Complicated Life

Though Mr. Wilkie was wheelchair bound,
He was free in his mind.
Even though now he has gone,
He's left a legacy behind.
A pioneer of Black Supplementary Education in Britain
To the powerful literary works he has written.
He will remain prominent in history, as in our hearts,
He has helped to put together a once Broken Britain
Piece by piece, part by part.
The vast bank of knowledge that he had to give
Has taught me one thing,
Live life simply, so others can simply live.

Balin Shah (15) 2013

Root to the fruit

Happy Memory

Root to the Fruit has been so fun
They included everyone
An experience I would gladly repeat
A memory I will treasure and keep.

But now it has come to an end
My sincerest thanks I would like to send
To the organisers who made it so great
10 out of 10 is how it would rate!

Lindsay Warner (14) 2011

Eyes

It's not what is in the mouth,
And it's not what is in your heart
It's the eyes that tell a story,
Look deep in the eyes,
To find out your future!

Henrietta Perry (14) 2011

Hiccups

The camera is rolling
What do I say?
I wish these hiccups
Would go away.

Time's running out
Am I doing okay?
It's just these hiccups
That will not go away.

The interview is over
Is that it for the day?
Thank goodness those hiccups
Didn't spoil the day.

Charlotte Corcoran (12) 2011

Root to the Fruit

History.
His story.
The elders once came to this land,
A lot of knowledge right in the palm of their hand.
All the knowledge rich from the source,
Some came here by choice, others by force,
And interview, a talk, some questions.
Some of them in rapid succession.
The world isn't as simple as it seems,
Some of their stories went to the extreme
A fact file of knowledge has now been uncovered,
And to me, it has been discovered
Pains, sorrows or happy times,
The elders are still in their prime,
So much has happened to them in such little time.
All of their lives coming at me like an articulated lorry,
It is history
His story
Her story
Our story.

Balin Shah (14) 2011

Root to the Fruit

From the very beginning
To the very end
You face the reality
Learn lessons

You can't go
Without giving something
As a form of anything
Or even a saying

You talk about life
You talk about strife (angry or bitter disagreement)
You can talk about anything
Just give a piece of advice

It's so nice
You can spend hours,
Which will seem like minutes,
When we talk about life

Views of the world
Views of the generation
Views of the society
Views of our thoughts

All about their story
We listen and learn
Difference between now and then
Their wisdom and know-how
The sacrifices they've done

Seeds they sow
We reap the fruit now
Older generation is the base
For our path ways
Now it's up to us
To do the same and make a new way

Sonam Ubhi (14) 2011

Root to the Fruit Interview

Rehearsing, waiting, shaking
Sitting down, knowing that I will be
In the interview room in the matter of seconds.
Reading, rehearsing again and again,
Butterflies flying around and around in my stomach.
Trembling in fear,
Standing up, walking, shaking.
After my name had been called,
My first steps into the interview room,
Standing behind the line
With my knees banging each other
Still waiting and shaking.
"Ring Ring!" went the interviewer's phone
Saved in the nick of time!
Practise fire alarm went off… saved again!
Asking my five questions, relaxed and calm
Asking my last question,
This experience is over!
Wonderful information I have gathered
We are really at the 'Root to the Fruit!'

Jasmine Shah (11) 2011

Root to the Fruit: Ethelca

I was the root who interviewed a fruit,
It was me and Ethelca that day.
She was the fruit and I was the 'youth'
Who made a little history that day.

A short documentary, set in the last century,
Caribbean to UK bound, Ethelca a worker
Never a shirker, made community and family,
Her life, although there was some trouble,
And some strife,
Ethelca held strong and never did wrong.
She kept to her own rhythm, her own song

Dominica Overseas National Association,
A most wonderful creation,
Which Ethelca Chaired with Grace.

Ethelca Brand you must understand,
A credit to the human race!

Cassius Callen-Jackson (11) 2011

The Interviewer

I don't think you can feel a feeling of splendour,
Than just finding out you are going to interview an elder.
The training it takes, the preparation the professionals seek,
Were "merely" children but I did it in over several weeks.

We went through the build-up, right to the techniques,
We did it in the end.
You can't stop WAPPY's poetry freaks!
Not freaks in a mean way, freaks of passion
Because we ride - down the success freeway.

After all the schooling
It was the day of interviewing,
It was the day I was 'rueing',
But I got it done and learned a new history
And learned a new past
My interview went well
I was happy at last!

Zion Duncan (12) 2011

*Ealing Gazette Pride in Our Ealing Nominees for Heritage Lottery Funded
The Root to the Fruit Project, 2011 & 2012*

Short, Sweet and Smiley

Ambition

I've got an ambition
I'm on a mission
To get in to my audition
I'll find out after my submission.

Ricari Wilson (10) 2017

Books

Books. We all read them
There's horror for a scare,
But if you dare!

Fiction for your imagination to go wild,
Mostly for a child.
But non-fiction for facts,
Some about hats!

Mohamed Ali (10) 2017

Fufu

You have it with soup,
It's a big white ball, with chicken or fish.

You have to wash your hands first,
Then you can start eating with your hand.
But don't use your left hand,
Or you will get licks.

Don't use a spoon,
It will taint the flavour.
Scoop up the meat with the fufu,
And scoop up the soup,
And eat.

If you don't finish it,
You will get more licks,
And an extra bowl to finish.

If you do finish it,
You will get more to eat.
So, eat it and enjoy.

Ben Eshun (12) 2011

Leila

Naughty, cheeky
Amusing, lovable, funny
Love to sing and dance a lot...
Beautiful!

Leilani Drummey (7) 2011

Mad Sam

Once upon a time,
There was man called Sam,
He was a mad man
And broke with no money
Because he was a silly billy.
He was a mad man!

Zephaniah Pascal (7) 2014

Man on the Moon

Hi, this is Bob
And my name is Bobby.
Every morning we get up at six o'clock.
Every morning we have a cup of tea and two eggs,
And leave for the rocket launch.
We are astronauts and every day we go to the moon,
We clean the moon every morning

Before we get to work.
And we do tricks,
Then we have a picnic on the moon.

Darcey Carter (9) 2013

Meteors and Dinosaurs

Dinosaurs, Dinosaurs
Scary as guns!
A wave of terror hits
If you see one!

Keegan Bloom (8) 2012

My New School

Massive, crazy
Makes me hazy
Project, produced
Makes me shout loudly, "HELP!"

Tamzin Chaman 2013

The Worst School in the World

School - let me out!
Big loud noise!
Playtime is the worst.
Assembly is boring
And all you hear from me is snoring!

Tamzin Chapman (9) 2013

Taller Than Tall

Building up power, building up might
Now all the bubbles are ready to fight
Unless you give it your all
The bubbles will be very small!

But even if you don't try
You will always have fun, fun, fun!
Let's have fun, let's be proud
Let's shout loud! Loud! loud!

Even if you don't give it your all
You must always stand
Taller than Tall!

T-Khai James-Palmer-Wahome-Kellehey (9) 2018

The day I went to Manchester

I went on a trip
Then I hurt my hip
I looked at the bruise and sighed
We got to the place
I fell on my face
Then I cried and cried and cried!

Mariam Allawi (6) August 2013

The Old Man of Peru

An old man of Peru
Thought he was eating his shoe,
Woke up in the night
And found it was perfectly true!

Amin Nabizada (6) 2014

There Was an Old Man from Leeds

There was an old man from Leeds
He found a colourful bead
And came up his luck,
He fell in the muck
And found a cheque in the reeds!

Tamzin Chapman (9) and Darcey Carter (9) 2013

The School of Fate

School sucks!
They have gunk for food.
I can't help but sleep,
Because it's work! work! work,
The teachers are so strict!

Kai Sim (9) 2013

Telling Tales

Artwork by Effie Quansah-George
2018

Across the Bridge

The billy goat crossed the bridge. He wanted to eat some green grass. The next billy goat also went across the bridge, but a troll called out,

"Who's that trip trapping across my bridge? I'm going to eat you up!!"

The big billy goat came and there was a big fight and they splashed into the water!

Tehannalee James-Palmer-Skeete (5) 2018

All About Treasure

"My mother!" I cried, as I found a lovely boxed filled with shiny, sparkly, diamond patterned earrings. The pattern on the box was white and had roses on the white bit of the lid. There was a circle with hearts on it.

When my mother saw it, her heart exploded!

"I love the box, it is colourful!"

Santanna Otalvora-James-Palmer (8) 2018

A Regular Christmas

"Don't look at me like that! It's a credit crunch, you know! Be festive!"

"I don't like the silence!"

"Whatever!"

"Let's watch the Queen's Speech then!"

"You mad! Me na want watch dat woman who are teef up the benefit."

"I am trying to practice here."

"The Angel Gabriel...[Singing]"

"Shhh Shhh, trying to open presents here!"

"Mmmm, socks. Wow! Just what I wanted! Great auntie, twice removed, haven't seen you in ten years. Jay, family guy. Box Set! That's what I'm talking about! Givey give."

"Oh, an IPod Touch Second Generation. Very nice. What is it?"

"Where's the beer?"

"People! Stop! Remember what Christmas is all about?"

"Santa, elves, food, beer?

"No! The Son of God.

"Who?"

"The hippie guy. You know, Oh, the Jesus dude?"

"What a myth! Just wait and see if Santa visits you today."

"Mmmm. I knew it!"

"What?"

"You gave me the socks?"

"Shut up!"

"Be quiet!"

"I'm trying to drink here!"

"What can I say?

A regular Christmas I guess........."

Georgiana Jackson-Callen (14) 2009

Christmas Mouse, Christmas Rabbit and Christmas Santa

Once Upon a Time it was Christmas day and Christmas Mouse woke up. It was nice and snowy, so mouse went to find his friend, Christmas Rabbit. He was opening his presents from Santa.

Christmas Mouse went to see if he had any presents but when he got there he was so sad. He had no presents under his tree. Mouse told Rabbit he wanted to tell Santa. They went to the North Pole where Santa lives. Mouse told Santa that he had no presents and Santa forgave him. They had hot chocolate with Marshmallows in it. They drank it and went in to his workshop to see his elves and how they were doing.

Santa asked Christmas Mouse what he wanted so Christmas Mouse whispered it in Santa's ears. Santa said to his elves,

"Make a cheese cake for my little Mouse friend here."

So, the elves made a gigantic cheese cake for Mouse. He gave everyone a piece, which was a kind thing to do.

Santa, Rabbit and Mouse went upstairs. They did puzzles, musical statues, musical chairs and watched TV. They had so much fun. It took a little while for them to come downstairs but at least they had so much fun. It was like a playdate. The best play date ever.

Finally, Santa said,

"Will you live with me forever!?"

Rabbit and Mouse nodded.

Sasha Vaughan (6) 2017

Diversity

One winter's day, a herd of stallions were playing in the mountains. They were having a lot of fun. But only one stallion could not run, jump, trot, gallop, canter or play. His legs were wobbly, ever since he was born, and all he could do was sleep, eat, watch the others use their legs, and lie down on a bed of straw.

The herd of stallions lived in the mountains, which were frosty white at the very top. There was heaps of snow. The little stallion felt very lonely. He was so unlucky, but his name was important and made him brave. Every other stallion teased him, but he didn't get offended.

The annual dance fair arrived, and he was the only one that couldn't come. The owls, the eagles, the hawks, the falcons and every other animal came, including the stallions. Little stallion couldn't come because of his legs but that was just because of diversity. He never really enjoyed his life, and this was the night that he least enjoyed in his life. But that is called diversity.

Adeola Aderibigbe (8) 2017

Evie

Once upon a time in a faraway land, there was a girl called Evie. She loved to read. One day, while she was reading, she fell into a hole. She saw the Queen of Hearts. They became friends.

Teagan Courtney (5) 2018

Jack and the School

A little boy named Jack, he really wanted to go to school but where he lived there was no such thing as 'school'. He was very upset and annoyed because his sister annoyed him, as she didn't let him have the PlayStation. He closed his eye for a few minutes and started to imagine what school was like.

Was is bright, coloured, and big, or was it dark, small and scary?

Laith Abed (4) 2018

Kja, Lola and T-Rex the Dinosaur

I went flying through the air and hit the ground with a thump. I stood up and looked at the strange surroundings. This was not home! It seemed to me that I had landed myself in a pre-historic period.

As I walked with no confidence at all, I spotted an extremely large dinosaur with a longer neck than a giraffe. With all the different extraordinary species to look at there was no time to be scared. After one hour of exploring the different things, I think, if I'm not mistaken a girl with brown hair and a large black bag on her bag appeared.

I decided to introduce myself. As I walked towards her, she started walking too, then we come face to face.

"Hello, what's your name?" I said.
"My name?" She replied. "My name is Lola," She added.
"Wow! What a lovely name!" I replied back, "My name is Kja."

We both strolled around this extraordinary landscape together but suddenly a herd of dinos came charging our way. We both screamed and ran to one side after a few minutes. Then the ambush was over, and both Lola and I wanted to know what it was. It was the great and mighty T-Rex!

All of a sudden the ground began to tremble and shake from the right corner. We both heard a tremendously loud roar, and from that moment on Lola knew exactly what it was. I ran as fast as I could but for some reason Lola stood there. It looked like she wanted it to eat her up.

The T-Rex bent down and with great strength ate Lola right before my eyes! I thought it was the end...It was the end!

For no reason at all a rush of anger ran over my body. I had to get her back, so I shouted, "Hey T-Rex! I'm getting my friend back whether you like it or not!"

So with all my strength I climbed up the muscular legs. Twenty minutes later, I finally reached the large mouth. All I had to do was make him roar. I flicked and kicked his ear until he let rip... "Roarrrr!"

I had just enough time to swiftly slip down his large gullet. I fell into a swimming pool of hot liquid. It was only then I realised I was in the stomach of a dinosaur-eating dinosaur! Sadly, I couldn't see Lola anywhere. The only thing left of her was a neck load of hair.

"But wait! That load of hair was Lola's!"....I grabbed hold of it and there she was!

"Lola, You're alive!"

"Yes, I was just searching for my torch."

"I'm so glad you're not dead!" I said joyfully.

We had to find a way out of here. We started climbing up T-Rex's oesophagus, but it was slimy. Lola came to the rescue; she had a rope. We tied it to a very weird dangly, thingy in his mouth and began to climb up. By the time we were both up all alone and really tired we just had to wait for him to open his mouth again.

It was only a matter of time when T-Rex finally opened his mouth. When he did both flew out, but rather than me going down with Lola, I went up and landed asleep in my bed.

Leila Drummey (8) 2018

Artwork by Walid Alqaddah

Outside My Window, 1966.

Dear Diary,

I had the most mysterious day I would ever have. That all started this morning. I was getting dressed for the day. When I was putting my shoes on, I looked out of my window. I saw a cloaked figure down below. His face was hidden by the hood, and his eyes were very mysterious. He only had one tooth.

I was afraid. I ran downstairs to tell my mum, but she didn't believe me, so I brought her upstairs. But then, when my mum and I came into my bedroom, the figure was already there. We didn't know what he was there for, but he said, "Put your hands up!" We put our hands up.

He stole our most prized possessions, and we called the cops. But we realised that the cops that came were phonies, and they'd kidnapped the real cops. We didn't know what to do! If he gets away with all our prized possessions, then that means fighting.

We ran downstairs and found the figure already there, just like we did in the room, and we started fighting. He lost his only tooth, and then we saw that figure was…my father!

My mum was very disappointed in him and called the real cops. She didn't know why he did it, but now he's going to get fired from his job. He was the chief of police, but he only wanted to get his hands-on money, like he was doing all the time that he was a cop. He just wanted money, money, money. But then, I broke my leg. I did a somersault and landed on it badly. I don't know how I did that somersault, but no one was controlling me. And then I woke up. And then I was in the hospital.

I hope to write in you again.

Adeola Aderibigbe (8) 2016

Penalties

FINALS!

The crowd whistled and screamed as I warmed up for the second half of the World Cup Finals. Suddenly, the referee blew his whistle and we were off! Kane passed it to the left winger, where Dele Ali was waiting. Ali dribbled up to the corner flag before crossing it into the box where I was waiting. Before I knew what was happening, my foot had stuck out and I had scored!

One nil to England. Ten minutes later Germany had unfortunately scored, making the score 1:1.

"Come on Team!" I shouted for motivation.

After fifteen more minutes both were yet to score again when "toot! toot! toooooot!" The referee's whistle went, signalling the end of the match.

But a World Cup Final never ends in a draw!

Penalties...

Riley Vaughan 2018

Servenap

Quite a long time ago there was a boat called Servenap. It lived for very long because it was great. When it was war time, the boat sank. One hundred years later 23rd June 2018, a lady called Sqanas discovered the ship and she renewed it and lived in it.

Nyah Walcott-Quansah (7) 2018

Sweet Story

Hello Ladies and Gentlemen,

Do you remember the days your mum put the sweets in the cupboard over night? I think you do. This is something that I remember from when I was five.

This is how the story starts....

I was in the kitchen begging my mum if I could stay up a little longer when I saw a sweet jump from the treat box onto the table and go still. Intrigued, I quickly pocketed it before my mum could notice and accepted that I was going to bed, because of the plan that was just beginning to create itself inside my young head.

The relief on my mum's face, when I had finally given in, was real, as she led me upstairs to my bedroom to fall asleep and dream. Unfortunately for her I had other plans than taking a nap....

So, I examined the sweet that I had seen jump to kill time, till I could hear my mum's distinctive snores after about half an hour. They very soon came so I crept downstairs and went to the kitchen.

To my disappointment, I found no jumping chocolate. Feeling let down, I turned to the door but immediately stopped in my tracks....I could have sworn that I had heard a faint rattling noise coming from the sweet cupboard.

Feeling the familiar curiosity take over I carefully climbed to the top of a chair and opened the cupboard door, a small crack, to see what was making the noise.

If you are wondering why I bothered to be careful about it, I want you to know that I was a timid and gentle girl, who was easy to scare so that's why I didn't rush.

The sight that I saw would not be easy to forget. What I saw was squelching wrappers, covering sweets that were leaping in and out of the box, as if they were doing a very carefully planned dance. I barely noticed my mouth, watering as I shot out my little hand to grab the orange sweet.

As I ripped of the plastic it jumped right onto the floor where it remained still. This time more cautious, I carefully approached it. But the other sweets in the cupboard caught my attention and I saw that they were jumping over each other like playing a game.

The sight was so peculiar that I laughed at it. It sounded loud and clear through the house. But as soon as it was out of my mouth (as you may expect) came in my angry-looking mum, and as soon as she came through the door all the colourful sweets went still.

From here, I am sure you can work it out, but I will say it anyway. My mum put me to bed and I woke up the next day as if nothing had ever happened!

Gerda Kleinberga (12) 2016

219

Tallulah

In this story you will find out about how a unicorn lost its horn.

One day a unicorn was getting ready to go to Greece and was packing her luggage. Very surprisingly, the unicorn was getting ready to board the plane when she suddenly noticed her horn was gone!!! She was screeching!

She then got to her hotel and fell asleep. The unicorn was upset the next morning.

Santanna Otalvora–James-Palmer (8) 2018

The Error

Many seconds ago, some random guy named Tom strolled casually into the deadly caves of Medusa. Here, there was no telling where the next trap would be.

Suddenly, Tom began to hear snakes and as he walked forward they began to get louder! This was it! He was so close. He slowly entered the room with his eyes closed. If he had them open, all he would be able to see was Medusa and the darkness.

"Hey Medusa!" Tom shouted.

"Ah", Medusa said, "Another weak, little mortal."

"Hey you!" Tom began to say, opening his eyes but before he could finish, he had turned to stone!

"Ha! Ha!!" Medusa laughed...

Riley Vaughan (10) 2018

The Flute

The crowd went wild as I played a wonderful tune. It was beautiful. The other people began to play a piano, violin, guitar, and trumpet. I was playing a green American flute, which was from Barbados.

The crowd whistled and cheered happily. Everyone was overexcited!

Sasha Vaughan (7) 2018

The Flying Scotsman

Once upon a time Nathan liked steam trains. He came to see the The Flying Scotsman. It was green, and it had a loud whistle, and it had sixty-eight carriages.

Nathan went on the train. It was nice and beautiful. But how much did it cost? It costed £478 to go on the steam train!

Then Nathan went off the train and went home.

Ashley Robert Halloween-Wadsworth (7) 2018

The Girl Who Liked Swimming

Once upon a time there was a girl who liked swimming and she swam with the fish. She came to the Lost City and made friends with the fish.

The End!

Talia Sokal (5) 2018

The Mythical Quest

Once upon a time there was a girl called Eve who wanted to go on a journey into the jungle, so she wondered if her friends wanted to come.

Eve asked her friends and they said, "yes." The next day, they went on the journey into the jungle. When they went further, they saw an immense dragon. Then they walked closer and closer until they saw that it was not a dragon. It had long wings and tiny feet and no nose. Then they walked past it. After that, they saw a huge cave.

When they entered, they saw a lot of gold. They saw some genies and the genies said,

"If you want to go on a real journey, then you must follow us."

So they followed the genies who took them into a mythical cave. When they entered they found a baby dinosaur egg. They ran back to the other dragon-like creature and it was actually the dragon-like creatures' baby. Then they ran back home.

Robyn Wisdom (8) 2018

The Necklace

"Here, my daughter," whispered my mother, gently handing me an antique necklace,

"I won't be around for long, my child, so I want you to have this as a reminder of me."

"Where will you go?" My nine -year-old self-questioned, placing the orange beaded necklace around my rounded neck.

"On a journey. One day. Just know my sleep will be long and heavy. Good night, my love. I will see you in a little while."

She kissed my head and walked away. She left to go to bed. I was the only one that woke up the next day...

Ivy Oppong (14) 2018

The Return of the Fish

One ordinary day in an ordinary way a frog came to annoy a fish.

"We meet again you filthy frog!" The fish muttered.

"Don't judge me, you flappy fish!" replied the frog. The fish and the frog were so hurt, they both swam away.

The next day in the blue, bubbly aquarium, the rest of the family of frogs came for a visit to the family of fish. Not long though, the fish and the frog started to fight, screeching extremely loudly and annoying everyone in the aquarium.

King Shark, however, was having none of it and he came to separate this tragic fight. Everyone stopped and watched. They both apologised and then everyone realised that they were peas in a pod for as long as the world goes on!

Mark Mwangi (7) and Effie Quansah-George (10) 2014

The Rope of Anansi

In 167 AD, a man named Konjo lived in Ghana with his children, Kuasa and Junior, his mother Niteri, and his wife Manuela. Konjo was a diamond miner and he earned quite a bit each day. He had a very nice house which he lived in with all his family.

One day while walking out of the mine he fell down a hole. A hole in the earth below him that began to crumble. As he fell everything was in slow motion. Everything went black.

For about five minutes Konjo was unconscious. When he woke up his vision was blurry. As he regained his vision his left arm was gone! But he felt a tug on what was left of his arm and out of the ground emerged a glowing red and blue rope. That rope wrapped itself around Konjo's arm and formed, well, a makeshift arm that felt real. The arm had a gold symbol that looked like a tarantula.

"Hello!" whispered a voice.

"Who was that?" asked Konjo.

"Anansi," replied the voice. "I gave you that rope. I saved your life and now you need to save your village."

"From what?"

"Haven't you heard? The war started six years ago!" Anansi said questioningly.

"Six years! Six years! You are telling me I have been a clown here for six years?"

"Yes, you have. Now you need to get out of here. Aim your new arm up at that opening" instructed Anansi.
Konjo did as he was told.

"Nothing's happening" argued Konjo.

"Oh yeah? Think so?" said Anansi.

"Uh...Ahhhhhhh!!"

The rope arm extended until it grabbed the edge of the hole. In less than five seconds he was up near the opening. As he walked out, he saw the destruction of what was left behind.

"What happened?" asked Konjo.

"The Donjigo clan."

As Konjo walked closer to his house, he realised that his family was gone...

"Manuela! Junior! Kuasa!" he yelled. "I will find you!"

Christian Ferguson-Dawkins (11) 2018

The Story of Annabelle

Once there was a doll named Annabelle who lived in a cellar of silky green goo. The luscious green goo swallowed people and then spat them out.

Present Day: There was a boy called Michael who lived with his mum and dad, Mr and Mrs. Greggs. One day he walked into the cellar and there it was Annabelle and the green goo. He was swallowed up and spat out. Since that day, Michael was cursed by Annabelle. Everywhere he went, he saw a glimpse of Annabelle and then she was gone...

Suddenly, a lightning bolt struck right in front of Michael and Annabelle was there. She shouted,

"You can't escape," in a creepy voice.

"No!" Michael cried, as she quickly grabbed him. She disappeared in a puff of smoke and Michael ran rapidly away from that area.

Annabelle was never seen again.

Anaya Murrell (9) 2018

The Very Sad Butterfly

Once upon a time there was a very energetic butterfly.
He adored the outside and had started reading when he was a
tiny caterpillar. Then he got stuck in a window.
He was very sad until Johnny rescued him.

The End

Finlay Sokal (7) 2018

避難所への信頼 Trust in Heaven

Four centuries ago lived the arrogant Machuki who loved hair and beauty products.

She lived in Osaka and was the most beautiful person in that city.

One day she was walking past one of the moats of the castle.

"Help!" She hears spluttering, screamed a boy,

"I shall not save him, I have put on new makeup, it will be ruined."

Well she did not want to do that as her selfishness got her a room in the prison,

Reinforced walls, guards at every cell and vile food.

Every night she prayed to Raiden God Thunder to destroy the walls, she also prayed to the even Japanese Gods of Luck.

One must have smiled upon him as after three years a dragon came.

It flew into the walls of her cell, grabbed her by in its talons.

For many days it flew, and it landed in front of a Lord, Lord Kamakura, they fell in love at once and were married within the week!

Luke Haenlein (12), Maddy Haenlein (10) and
Daniel Alawode (7) 2011

Water Free

Dear Diary.

There was a little girl called Evie who lived in the ocean and she went into a cave and saw a new ocean. When she got in the ocean, she turned into a mermaid! She felt very shocked because she wanted to keep it a secret.

Evie had three friends. One of them was called Lizzie. "You have to keep this a secret!" she said.

So off they went to follow Lizzie into the cave.

Her eyes were wide open, and she said,

"How can I turn into a mermaid?"

So Evie said,

"Just jump in!"

Lizzie jumped in and then turned into a mermaid.

Tristan Wisdom (7) 2018

Where Do I Belong

Artwork by Sara Abed
2012

Don't Judge Me!

It was hard times for my African ancestors
Who were enslaved, the African Holocaust.
It was hard times for the European victims
Of the Jewish holocaust

Is it wrong for me to love my own?
Is it wrong for me?
Is it wicked that my skin is black?
Because my mother is native American Indian?
Because I was born where my mother lived?
Because I died for my people and my country?
Because I am known by my native name?
'GITCHI MANIDOO WARRIOR EAGLE'
Don't judge me at all!

Kieran Ross (15) 2012

Here Forever

The Windrush, not where it started,
WW2, not where it started,
Thousands of years ago, that's where it started,
Africa to England, Africa to America
The long boat ride which blacks fulfilled
Thousands of years ago,
That's where it started
At least for the most of us,
Some of us, we're here forever!

Riley Vaughan (11) 2018

I Don't Care!

I don't care whether you are black like creamy chocolate,
I DON'T CARE!
Whether you are white like snow,
I DON'T CARE!
Whether you are mixed race like a potato,
Guess what?
I DON'T CARE!
Because it doesn't matter what colour you are!

Kai Sim (7) 2011

I know Where I Belong

My Heritage is British
I am ten years old
My skin colour is mixed race
And I like to stay paced
I walk into the playground and I realise
It is not what you look like
But what your character is
So, I no longer worry where I'm placed,
Black, British, I don't care
It's about that flair,
The personality inside there.

Jai Ellis (10) 2010

Illusions

Like a watercolour painting
You look better from far away.
Your life's like a full moon; magnificent
But slowly beginning to wane.

Surrounded by people but still lonely
Wrapped in cashmere but still cold
Smiling outwardly but crying inside
Looking youthful but becoming old.

So, that's the life of Riley?
Who's Riley anyway?
Some snob with more money than sense
Living greedily from day to day?

No, that life isn't for me,
All diamonds and dresses and pearls.
Me, I prefer t-shirts and jeans;
I'm just an Acton girl.

Georgiana Jackson-Callen (13) 2008

Leika

I'm Lovely like cuties
I'm excellent as a hero
I'm imaginative like a storyteller
I'm kind as a good girl
I'm amazing as a star

Leika Boundy (7) 2011

Malaysian Grand Sun

I feel like I am meant to be in Malaysia,
The sun shining,
Not a cloud in the big, blue sky!

Where my dad's mum and dad's dad live
And in Chinese, my sister and I
Call them 'Ah Mah' and 'Ah Kong'.

The sun beams of boiling gold,
Shooting down on us and burning our skin
As red as blood.

Kai Sim (8) 2012

Me

My name is Miriam.
I am 8 years old.
I come from England.
I was born in London.
I am a fairy.
I wish I was born in Egypt.
I speak Arabic.
I love going to climb in the park.
I love eating sweets.
I am good at swimming.
I want to be a dentist or a doctor.

Miriam Mikhaeil (8) 2012

Mixed Race: Isn't Just Black and White

Mixed race isn't just black and white
Nor the colour of your face.
History isn't just about your past,
It's your future and what you portray.

Mixed race isn't just black and white,
It's the personality inside,
Not the person
On the other side

Mixed race isn't just black and white,
Nor is it subject to discrimination
All you do is bring disgrace
To yourself and your nation

Mixed race isn't just black and white,
It's other colours too!
So, stop and think….
What does mixed race mean to you?

Shahidah Victor Sampson (15) 2011

My Grandma and Me

I am from Africa,
But I have an 'Up North' accent.
My Grandma Monica tells me
Interesting facts about Africa.
I sit there and think
What questions I could ask her.
She says Africa is a nice place,
And a very poor place too.
I love her, and can you guess what?
She loves me too.

Grace Simons (7) 2011

My Mother's Arms

A sanctuary place, a safe place, a warm place.
A place where no one can touch me,
Mother's arms.
My mother's soft and silky arms.
My mother's wise and gentle, soft and caring.
Once in my mother's arms I'm covered by a shield.
I couldn't be more safe.

Maisa Abed (12) 2013

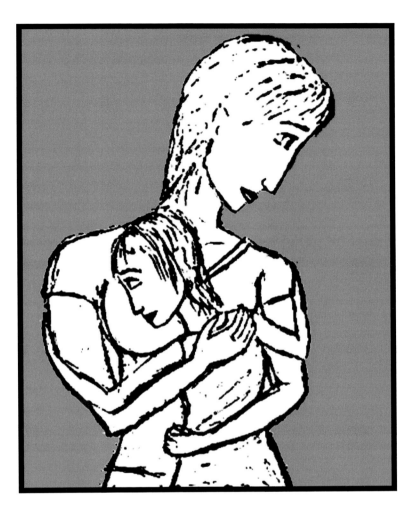

Artwork by Maisa Abed
2012

Parents

They seem presidential because they own you.
They are attached, because they love you.
They rule you, because they just do!
Ecstatic, when you make them proud.
Your parents would never give up on you.
Throughout your life,
They are always there for you.
They keep you safe,
They keep you warm,
They guard you from every harm.

Julia Baramo (13) 2013

St Lucia

My name is Jessica
And I have travelled to St Lucia
When I was a baby.
I live in London.

London is a fascinating
And a good place to live.
Some people are black,
Some people are white.

A few years ago,
I went to St. Lucia
And I went to my grandfather's house.
I had lots of fun.
The people are beautiful.
The place is beautiful.
We are all beautiful!

Jessica Bruley (6) 2011

The Coconut Disaster

I am made up of lots of bits -
A little bit Welsh,
A little bit Chinese,
A little bit Malaysian.
But we are all created by God.

When we drink Coconut Milk,
Sometimes people don't like it.
I don't hate people who don't like Coconut Milk.

We are all different.
And God makes new things for the world ...
The whole time!

Seren Sim (5) 2011

Tiny Torquay

It started off with a trek on a train
So many people, it was hurting my brain,
Driving me insane.

Finally finishing the rollercoaster ride,
Luckily, our hotel was only to the left side!

Day 1... Had me feeling cold and funny,
Day 2... Chilling at the beach, it was kind of sunny.

Day 3... Crash! Boom! Bang! We heard a noise,
It was the wicked witch laughing next door!
As the storm started the rain pelted on the floor.

Day 4... Leaving the tranquil island,
The setting around us was stunning like Thailand.

The rollercoaster arrives at our final destination,
Turning around to go back is such a temptation.

From London to Torquay, and Torquay to London
Tiny Torquay left us feeling abandoned...

Shania Bajaj (14) and
Effie Quansah-George (14) 2018

Two Boys from Ealing

We are Two Boys from Ealing
Who like jumping off the ceiling,
We do this only at WAPPY
Because it keeps us happy.

Today is our first day,
So far it's been okay.
We like to ride our bikes in Ealing,
So we can practice our wheeling,
But definitely, not on the ceiling

These are our first WAPPY verses,
And they have no curses
Our next poem will not be for free.,
We'll charge you a £5 fee!

Isaiah Ansah (11) and Louis Leeson (11) 2017

Wonderful World of Wappy

INSIDE WAPPY'S WORLD BY STAFF, PARENTS & FRIENDS

Artwork by Athena Ioannou
2018

MY FAVOURITE MEMORIES

I started in 2008, acting as administrator, later interim treasurer, trustee and now trustee advisor.

My favourite memories are of seeing past WAPPY members developing their talents and going on to follow their chosen paths, of past and present trustees and workshop volunteers, and of some great WAPPY presentations at prestigious cultural events.

Of course, Benjamin Zephaniah's visit to WAPPY in 2014 is a standout, as well as the launch of WAPPY's first anthology, 'The Soul of a Child' at the Huntley Conference in 2011; the 5th anniversary celebration at Hanwell Library in 2013, and the intensive Kyria Consulting training course leading to WAPPY's transformation as a social enterprise and registration as a company, also in 2013.

It's good to remember too, the pride on the faces of parents after seeing Showcase performances, and the obvious sense of achievement of the young writers and performers themselves.

My highlights are around music - the tribute to Michael Jackson, the research for the Bob Marley 70th anniversary celebration, and more recently the Bob Dylan Showcase and the enthusiastic response it received - as always with WAPPY, leaving everyone wanting more!

John Durston
Volunteer from 2008 & Trustee from 2013, WAPPY Parent, 2016

248

A GREAT OPPORTUNITY

It's very hard to choose a favourite event as I have enjoyed all of them. I think that I would pick the Bob Dylan Showcase that we had recently because it had a good turnout, but wasn't too big, and the local MP, Rupa Huq, Tim Beckerley (caretaker of a primary school in West London and children's poet), Eric Huntley, Jack Shalloo (Actor) and The Mayor of Ealing were in attendance. Acquaye's steel band music was fabulous.

The calibre of the poems read out by the children touched my heart, seeing the children perform so confidently with singing, interviewing, the amazing artwork, was warming and so much fun to see and be part of. Drawing out the creativity from children is important and gives so much to us all. I felt that the children there were also proud of themselves. A happy, inspirational event.

I am proud to have been a part of WAPPY right from the start. I have gone from having a conversation with Grace in my living room about the need for somewhere for children to be encouraged to write and be creative, to taking my own young children along to the WAPPY sessions. As a single parent with two young ones who needed a lot of stimulation and had a thirst for learning, it was enjoyable and helpful. My children grew in confidence and bonded with the other members of the group. They were given opportunities like making sculptures, meeting The Mayor of Ealing and Benjamin Zephaniah, performing their work on stage, attending a writing workshop at Keats's House, etc.

I felt privileged to be chosen later on to become a Trustee and be more involved in taking WAPPY forward and seeing other children given opportunities to learn and have fun at the same time. It was a great opportunity to give something to the community and to do a useful training course, after I had to give up my job as a Housing Officer because of personal difficulties.

My children are grown up now but still enjoy WAPPY events and are still friends with the WAPPY members they met. It was lovely to see my daughter volunteer this summer for the WAPPY Building Bridges Project.

Carolyn Warner
WAPPY Parent from 2008 & Trustee from 2013

A PLACE OF EXPRESSION WITHOUT BOUNDARIES

In 2009, simply put I said to Grace that she has created something that is powerful and will impact young lives beyond. 10 years later you continue to grow and now you reap the rewards of your drive. You are an inspiration!

WAPPY represents positive powerful energy channelled amongst volunteers and participants in a nurturing environment. It is a place of fun. It is a home of creativity. It is a place of expression without boundaries. WAPPY makes me want to smile. It makes me want to dance. It makes me want to be.

Benson Chinenzura
Workshop Assistant Volunteer 2009

A PLACE OF CREATIVITY WITHOUT BORDERS

WAPPY is a place for creativity without borders and gives the next generation of children coming through a wonderful focus. It has been a great honour to serve as both friend and Trustee to WAPPY.

Several years back, in 2009, I ran a workshop on the theme of 'Lost and Found,' which yielded thoughtful, humorous and hard-hitting poetry and fiction. Then to hear their words in performance added another dimension.

Another memorable reading was held at the London Metropolitan Archives, Farringdon on the theme of 'Hard Times in London.' It was 2012, the riots that preceded it were fresh in the mind and the Olympics were looming. The writing reflected their stories from across a multi-cultural London and signs of a city of growing inequality. Their voices formed a poetic choir, "Stereotypes of Young People Under Pressure" and the line, by Michael Larbi,

"I often hear of old people say, 'back in my day' but no offence this is my day!" was met with both laughter and applause."Watching them grow older and confident in their own expression has been an absolute delight. Their creative practice is bearing fruit as they go forward in their lives and long may it continue do so with the root and branch support of WAPPY.

Anjan Saha
2009 WAPPY Collaborator & Trustee, 2013- 2018

VIVA WAPPY!

I first volunteered with WAPPY in 2011 as a workshop assistant. Wow! Where to begin! I have lots of good memories but my favourite one is the Benjamin Zephaniah event at Ealing Central Library in 2014, which was fantastic, and it was a pleasure to have him there. It is good to see WAPPY expanding, and how it's giving young people the chance to open up and have their say about their feelings in poetry.

My role in WAPPY has been to help with organisation in the workshops, accompany the children on visits and as well as assist with catering in community events.

I am very grateful to WAPPY because I have made new friendships and gained a loving family, and I look forward to giving more support to WAPPY.

Rahwa Ghergish
Workshop Assistant, 2011-2018

A REWARDING AND INVALUABLE LEARNING EXPERIENCE

My affiliation with WAPPY began with my daughter, Jai, who joined tentatively at age nine, initially a shy individual. I continued to encourage her to attend and to contribute more. Jai's confidence grew slowly with each poem, rhyme and story written, from 'one liners' to group participation, 30 seconds solo song parts to singing sets of whole songs written by herself. My closeness to WAPPY grew naturally while supporting Jai, from participating in outings, visits and facilitating small creative workshops as a volunteer, to taking part in community training and spending a brief time on the Board of Trustees.

WAPPY has been a rewarding and invaluable learning experience for both me and Jai, and it's wonderful to witness the organisation go from strength to strength.

Marcia K Ellis
WAPPY Parent of one participant from 2009 & Trustee from 2013-2012

A CREATIVE COLLECTIVE OF TALENT, INSPIRATION AND POSSIBILITY!

I first volunteered with WAPPY in September 2014 as a Workshop Assistant and I have seen a considerable amount of change since that time. My favourite memory remains the Benjamin Zephaniah event at Ealing Central Library - a creative collective of talent, inspiration and possibility! To have such a spectacular showcase within my first month at WAPPY was simply marvellous.

From Building Bridges and the Bob Dylan Showcase to the Bob Marley 70th Birthday Tribute, there have been countless opportunities for the WAPPY family to create and present their own works.

In early 2018, I became a WAPPY Trustee and I hope that Grace, John and the entire team shall continue to serve and enrich you and your local communities."

Manjinder Chijarh
Voluntary Workshop Assistant 2014 -2017, Trustee 2017-2018

RAW INSPIRATION

My favourite memory is the WAPPY workshop in collaboration with The Story So Far, listening to the story of the 'Anansi/Nancy the Spider' told by Grace. At story time (in Southall Library) I remember sitting in a circle with all the children. Then Grace laid out colourful fabric, an instrument and a funny looking toy spider.

I was ready to be inspired. She proceeded to retell the story of Anansi and 'Nancy' to wide eyes. I love this old story and I enjoyed it so vibrantly told in a magical and artistic manner.

In terms of my overall experience, I really enjoyed the depth and innocence of the children's poems. They come up with funny, touching and meaningful stories. The children's point of views and inspirations are totally refreshing. This energy was also found as the children would tell stories through their drawings too. The raw inspiration and immediacy of the children's words could be very emotional and thought-provoking as the world of the child is so present. I hope I helped provide a comfortable space for the children to work and be supported in doing so.

Esther Ramnath
Volunteer Workshop Assistant 2014-2015

WAPPY OPENS UP OUR KIDS' HEARTS

I have been Trustee and Treasurer for WAPPY since 2014. It's been a great journey, watching WAPPY expand and help young people to open up their creativities.

WAPPY has inspired a lot of children including both my kids, Christopher (14) and Athena (7), who have attended events and workshops and they both showed so much potential. Christopher wrote a poem about Bob Marley during a workshop, which is very moving and made me so proud!

Both kids also attended some Building Bridges workshops, Walpole Park 5 Aside, and they joined a trip to see School of Rock Musical May 2018. They built amazing boats out of cardboard and other materials and learned so much about Spanish art and Christopher Columbus. In addition, they recently joined in a Rounders and a Picnic Day at Gunnersbury Park in West London (August 2018), as well as designed their own customised T-shirts and Inspirational customised postcards, which WAPPY printed them out for them!

In all the above WAPPY events, apart from having fun, they've had a great impact on the growth of my kids' confidence. I really appreciate Akuba's hard work and positive attitude which is so contagious. We're all hoping that WAPPY is going to organise more events. My kids and their peers would love to join more WAAPPY workshops. A huge thanks to WAPPY. I will be grateful forever!

Regina Ioannou
Treasurer/Trustee 2014, June 2018 & Parent of two WAPPY participants

A PLACE WHERE NEW FRIENDSHIPS ARE CONNECTED

I have been working with WAPPY as treasurer/trustee since June 2018.

WOW! Where to begin! For the short period that I have been involved within the team and have seen some of the projects on the internet, of what they have accomplished over the past 10 years, I could not be prouder and more honoured to be part of WAPPY.

My role is looking at the financial aspects and also to demonstrate the ability to assist in the workshops, when possible, which have been in the borough of Ealing. Kids from other boroughs (e.g. Islington) such as my own children are also able to take part and learn Spanish through Art, compose poems, do fun games as well as go on an outing such as to see the School of Rock Musical in May of this year, where all kids including mine were so happy at the end of this event.

WAPPY is not just a community for youngsters but also a place where new friendships are connected between parents, staffs and children from different backgrounds, creating this wonderful place which I can see also as family.

Marie Ikong Ehuy
Trustee 2018 & Parent of two WAPPY participants

INGENUITY OF THE YOUNGSTERS

I started volunteering with WAPPY from May 2018, when I helped out at the 'Dance & Games Day' session at St. Dunstan's Church and then was invited by Grace to jointly deliver an Arts & Spanish workshop, as I am both of Spanish heritage and a Fine Artist, with an interest in Realism. That session gave me the opportunity to exhibit my own pictures. In this session I have seen the ingenuity of the youngsters who took park. They were encouraged to ask questions and to understand Spanish translations of English words which related to the session, and they produced artwork, stories and designer T-Shirts inspired.

My favourite memory which I remember and still makes me laugh is when, during the Games Day workshop, we played 'Tug of War' in the gardens. It was a great game with two different teams. Grace joined one team that had lost the first challenge and she pulled so much stronger than the opposing team and her team won the next challenge. That was really good. I really enjoyed it!

Gloria Triguero-Bustamante
Volunteer Workshop Assistant 2018

A TRUE PRIVILEGE TO BE PART OF THIS JOURNEY.

I began participating in WAPPY sessions when I was quite young, but I still remember how excited I was to have a space that encouraged creative writing for the sake of writing, not just to fulfil part of a curriculum as it was in my school setting. It offered me the unique experience of performing my creative work in front of an audience, which has come in handy, as I have now gone on to study English Literature at university and perform my work more regularly in front of my academic peers. Now, having gone from a WAPPY member to a WAPPY volunteer, I have seen how the organisation has flourished and developed from those early sessions with a new generation of children. It has been a true privilege to be part of this journey.

Lindsay Warner
WAPPY Member 2009 - 2014, Volunteer 2018 & Editor 2018

WAPPY families and friends

....

10 YEARS AND GROWING STRONG

It seems like only yesterday when Grace came to me with what I felt at the time was a proposal unlike any other in the Borough at the time. It was a big "Yes" from Sarqi, John, Damien, David and me, almost immediately.

What a journey it's been. The laughter, the talented children, the fun, the efforts to make small fundings work big miracles and through it all, we never gave up. With Grace at the helm and Positive Awareness Charity in the background, guiding firmly with quiet unwavering determination, WAPPY has now become a fully-fledged Charity in its own rights. Well done and long may WAPPY continue to prosper.

Ifilia Francois
Coordinator of Positive Awareness

WAPPY'S VISION FROM A BEACH IN GHANA

I know that Grace shared the vision of WAPPY with me on the beach in Nzima, in the western region of Ghana in July 2007 whist we were holidaying there, and that Lifeline Learning Centre played a key role in the beginning of WAPPY. Lifeline provided a self-contained, safe space from the outset for WAPPY to run its workshops, and as it grew, in 2012 I recommended to Grace and John that they should approach Kyria Consulting for organisation support to help them become autonomous. With Kyria's intervention they did succeed with two successive funding applications and were able to transform WAPPY's structure to become a limited company.

I'm also delighted at the way Jai, a member I've known from her infancy, blossomed from the shy, retiring child to the confident artist and composer which has been partly due to the experience of WAPPY.

Judy Wellington
Principal of Lineline Learning Centre

AN HONOUR TO WORK WITH WAPPY

Working with Grace and the WAPPY team has been an honour seeing how much pleasure literature, writing poetry and stories has brought to children, parents and local community.

Grace has always passionate about working with young people and when first approached I remember thinking the pitch was exciting and different. We had nothing like this in libraries and I recall Grace's desire to disprove the idea that children and young people were no longer interested in reading and writing stories. I think everyone would agree that WAPPY has disproved that many times over. For Libraries the highlights over the 10 years were Benjamin Zephaniah at the Central Library and the wonderful Bob Marley and Bob Dylan events, with their associated poetry contests and exhibitions, which have led to creation of outstanding poetry and artwork. But more importantly we also celebrate the tireless work and commitment that Grace and the volunteers give every week at the writing workshops and the showcase events.

The partnership with WAPPY has brought in communities that would not normally visit the library and discover the services we offer. We have worked together to make joining and accessing library services as simple as possible. Well done Grace and the team and looking forward to celebrating the 20th Anniversary.

Martha Lambert
Reading Development Manager, 2018

10 YEARS OF WRITING, ACTING AND PUBLISHING PROJECT FOR YOUNGSTERS

WAPPY is a name that makes people smile before they even know any-thing about the organisation. It's so close to HAPPY, but zanier, that it triggers an immediate, inadvertent smile from everyone who hears it. "Wa... who?" They query. WAPPY and then you follow with the full description of the group.

I'm very happy to have been there at the beginning to support the group with funding from London Metropolitan Archives to publish your first collection of poetry. You have never looked back. But then you're guided by, Grace, someone whose enthusiasm for life matches the youngest and most energetic of you and what everyone gets is that you are all confidently, doing amazing things. You're interviewing major writers, you're reading confidently in public, you're writing poetry with the ease that other young people eat cornflakes.

Every time I've worked with you at the many locations throughout the City of London has been memorable. I've worked with you in the Guildhall, at Keats House Museum, in London Metropolitan Archives, Ealing Library and several community centres in Ealing. You're often good, very good, but most times you are amazing. I hope that going forward you will all realise the value of this amazing network. I'm waiting for our first WAPPY... member of parliament, young poet laureate? I know it's going to happen.

Happy Anniversary.

Maureen Roberts
Senior Development Officer, London Metropolitan Archives

WAPPY @ 10

Over the last ten-years I have had the pleasure to witness young people join the WAPPY family where they were nurtured to gain in confidence, encouraged to express themselves, supported to perform. With a passion to promote the achievements of young people, the organisers led by Grace Quansah, have determined to celebrate their contributions and achievements. ARTification has worked closely with WAPPY throughout, providing a platform for young writers and offering performance opportunities. It has been wonderful seeing the journey of the young people. We look forward to your future achievements.

Happy birthday WAPPY!

Dr Rachel Pepper
ARTification Director

"WAPPY has given my son, Zion, the inspiration to believe that his thoughts on paper made that validation possible. Thank you WAPPY."

TUUP
The Unorthodox, Unprecedented Preacher

Akuba with Rachel Pepper & TUUP
W3 Gallery 2018

WAPPY'S Impact on its Early Pioneers

....

ALLOWED ME TO CONNECT WITH PEOPLE FROM ALL WALKS OF LIFE

I was quite a shy child growing up, always wanting to stay in the background and never wanting to take the limelight. When I decided to do the WAPPY summer workshop, I was able to express myself through poetry. WAPPY allowed me to connect with people from all walks of life and allowed me to express myself in a warm and loving environment.

When I performed my poem, it gave me the opportunity to have the limelight for myself and gave me a platform to express myself freely to an audience.

To this day, the time I had spent at WAPPY will always be one my fondest memories.

With the skills I gained from WAPPY, I now walk with my head held high and with a confidence that I did not have before doing this workshop.

Shanice Coleman *(2008)*

A SUPPORTIVE COMMUNITY WHERE YOUNG PEOPLE CAN SHINE

I am an Acton girl first and foremost, and so very proud to be a founding member of WAPPY.

As a high performing student I acutely felt the pressures of GCSEs and A-Levels throughout my time at Twyford CE High School. A weekly two-hour session at WAPPY was enough not only to alleviate these pressures but also to provide me with a creative space where I could put my thoughts into words. Throughout my schooling I have seen too many of my friends burn out from the hamster wheel of work, stress and more work; WAPPY provides a safe, non-judgmental space where young people can create and enjoy guidance from a diverse range of mentors.

In fact, diversity is, without a doubt, WAPPY's star quality - and not just in its members and volunteers, who come from across generations, cities and ethnicities, but also in terms of skills gained and honed. For example, as a senior member who had previous experience in film, I was commissioned to film the WAPPY showcase a few years ago. This involved organising interviews with individual members, deciding on camera angles, capturing sound and finally editing it all together - a wonderful experience for a 15-year-old.

And finally, our valiant leader, Grace Quansah, goes by many names but none of them accurately capture what she truly is: a dynamo. I have seen her turn a group of children who are complete strangers into a group of firm friends able to create an original and coherent performance in the space of two hours. She is an absolute inspiration who really knows how to bring out the best in each member, leads a wonderful team of volunteers and raises WAPPY's profile by organising performances at venues such as Keats House - which proved massively helpful for my A-Level English - and most recently, in front of Benjamin Zephaniah himself. Added to numerous publications of members' poetry and prose, it is clear that WAPPY nurtures not only the personal but also the professional development of its members.

In conclusion, WAPPY is more than simply a Writing, Acting, Publishing and Performing Group for Youngsters: it is a briiant, phenomenally supportive community where young people can shine. I believe that every child in the Ealing area should have the opportunity to be part of such a community, and as such, there is no other cause I can think of that is more worthy of your support."

Georgiana Jackson-Callen *(2008 - 2015)*
Former Choral Scholar French and Spanish Undergraduate,
Merton College, Oxford and Proud alumna of WAPPY

PROVED THE TEACHERS WRONG

WAPPY was to me a place for a kid who lived quite a stifled existence to express freely. It was a place to learn that writing how I felt made things a little bit better. It was a place where I learned that a lot of the things I wouldn't have dreamed of were within reach.

Getting published gave me a confidence in an English classroom where they were predicting I was going to get a 'C' at GCSE. The end of that story is I got an A* and proved the teachers wrong.

I always loved reading but WAPPY showed me I could be the person who wrote things that people love reading. I'm 21 now and I write all the time now for my blog, email list, copywriting.

It's my bread and butter now!

Michael Larbi *(2008 - 2015)*

HELPED ME TO THINK OUTSIDE THE BOX

When I was asked to participate in WAPPY 10 years ago, in all honesty, I did it for my beloved mother rather than for me. I did not have the enthusiasm at the time. But in time I learned to appreciate the value of what it brings to young people. I have seen how much WAPPY has inspired other children to express themselves in ways they never did. It has also helped me with the ability to 'think outside the box' and has given me a greater insight with my creative writing. It has helped me improve on my vocabulary and it has made me more use to performing in front of an audience.

I have also met some great talented people from WAPPY, some of whom, I occasionally keep in contact with. I believe, I'm also the most published member, with my poems published in, 'A Lime Jewel (2010, Haiti fundraiser), 'The Soul of a Child' (2011), and 'Sweet Beats for Keats'. Taking all these details into account, I think the best compliment I can say is that I have no regrets about joining WAPPY.

Acquaye McCalman
Musician and Artist (2008-2018)

PUSHED ME OUT OF MY COMFORT ZONE

"As a shy girl at age nine, WAPPY provided me with a platform and gave me the confidence to perform my own material in front of an audience. It pushed me out of my comfort zone and allowed me to develop into the singer-songwriter I am today."

Jai Blue *(2009-2018)*

MY PUBLISHED POEMS ARE NOW 'OUT THERE'

I started WAPPY when I was six, in 2009, partly because my mum was running the sessions. I was probably the youngest unofficial member. But then I started writing, when I took part in the 'Lost & Found' summer workshops, which I enjoyed as I got to do some acting with older members and perform in front of a live audience.

I've done lots of work in WAPPY and it helps me with my English work at school. In fact, I'm WAPPY's longest member, and have been published several times, for example, my poem 'Haiti' is in The Soul of a Child (2011) and 'An Anansi Warning' is in Anansesem - a Ezine run in the Caribbean and in the Scrumbler (both, 2012). I've also performed at different places and have appeared in the local Ealing Gazette.

WAPPY's been going for ten years now and many more different children and students are joining, It's agreat organisation that has helped me. My highlight is when we performed My Favourite Idol at Twyford High School as part of the Spotlight Festival (2010) and I danced to Michael Jackson's 'Want You Back'.

Two of my favourite poems are 'An Anansi Warning' and 'Goodbye Walking, Hello Crutches'. The last one I performed at Acton Library in 2015 while on crutches, after breaking my toe. It has attached 560 views on Utube, and I also performed it at a Grenadian Foundation Sunshine Fundraising event in London (2015). Because of my poems published by WAPPY and performed publicly some of my work is 'Out There.'

Effie Quansah-George *(2009-2018)*

I OWE A LOT OF THE SUCCESSES I'VE HAD IN LIFE TO WAPPY

After facing a lot of ups and downs in my life due to having cancer at such a young at the age of four years, my WAPPY family has given me the opportunity to express the way I write my poetry from my personal expressions as well as experience. WAPPY always lets me be myself and share different ideas with many unique young people, like myself, to come together, regardless of our backgrounds.

WAPPY also gives young people a mini- sense of a spotlight of fame to produce unique talents within themselves. Within this generation I feel most young people are lost because these days there are a lot of negative images from music, drugs and some influences from friends or the environment. However, WAPPY gives you that good vibe which can be respect, peace, energy, confidence and a once in a lifetime experience. My favourite part of making poetry is to have the ability to transform your emotions into sound or energy as well through a poem. If I'm feeling happy or sad I can make a poem or song or about it, and use them to connect with people and to share my energy and vibes as well as raise my inner spirit.

I joined WAPPY at the young impressionable age of 12, and it has moulded me into the person I am today. 10 years on from joining WAPPY I'm pleased to have started studying medicine, a dream I've had since I was a little boy. It's been a long and tough road to get where I am today, and I feel like WAPPY and Grace have helped me throughout this journey. I can honestly and proudly say that I can credit many of the positive traits I have to WAPPY. The opportunities WAPPY has given me, such as being able to perform some of my written work has taught me how to come out of my shell, and I feel like it's helped me become the confident, driven person I am today. The continued support of Grace has assured me that no matter what I do in life, I'll have WAPPY to guide me. I owe a lot of the successes I've had in life to WAPPY and could not imagine where I would be if I didn't join them all those years ago.

Balin Shah *(2009-2013)*

A UNIQUE PLATFORM FOR YOUNGSTERS TO EXPRESS THEMSELVES

As one of the original members it is impressive to see how far the group has grown and matured over the years. This is no doubt owed greatly to the sustained passion and dedication shown by Grace and the other hard-working members of the committee.

WAPPY provides a unique platform for youngsters to express themselves through poetry and the performing arts outside of an academic environment, which is too often known to hinder creativity. Through various workshops and collaborations, such as the sculpture Carl Gabriel and the poet/professor Benjamin Zephaniah, a plethora of educational opportunities are afforded to children that would otherwise be out of reach.

I was fortunate enough to attend events at Keats House and The London Metropolitan archives and given the chance to read out some of my work. I found these experiences to be hugely impactful both in terms of confidence building and expressiveness. I very much hope that WAPPY continues to expand and keep being the brilliant social hub for learning and expression that has served the community over the last decade.

Nathan Warner *(2008-2018)*

NOTES ON CONTRIBUTORS

Grace Quansah *(Akuba) Editor*
is a former university lecturer, British Museum facilitator, performance artiste, writer, TalentEd GCSE Tutor, and Save Ealing Libraries' campaigner. Her achievements include 'Aspiring Female Storyteller' (Black Women in the Arts, 2006/2007), and winner of 'Random House Children's Books' writing competition (2006). 'The Awakening of Elmina' is published in Malorie Blackman's, Unheard Voices (2007). Published in 21 different collections including Journeys Home (US, 2009), her recent poem, 'Bittersweet Carnival' (a tribute to Grenfell Tower tragedy) was shortlisted by Benjamin Zephaniah in Hillingdon's 3rd annual Literary Festival Writing Competition and is published in 'Ordinary People/Exceptional Lives', 2017. In 2008, she founded Writing, Acting and Publishing Project for Youngsters (WAPPY), which develops the writing, artwork and performance skills of young people, with opportunities for performance, exhibition and publication. In 2011, she co-edited WAPPY's debut anthology, The Soul of a Child, with Maureen Roberts, (Bogle L'Ouverture Publications), and in 2015, with Eric Huntley, she co-edited, Mame Nwia-Amah, by Esther Ackah (Way Wive Wordz). She currently tours schools and heritage sites with her Marcus Garvey-inspired educational resource, Unpacking That Trunk', based on her father's work with the Ghanaian shipping liner, the Black Star Line.

Eric Lindbergh Huntley *Patron*
Eric Huntley is an author, educationalist, political campaigner, co-publisher and one of WAPPY's patrons. With Jessica Huntley, his wife, (now deceased), they founded radical book publishers, Bogle L'Ouverture Publications (now a community interest company) and have been proactively involved with the British African - Caribbean community's experience since their first arrival in England in 1956 to the 2010.

For over 50 years both Eric and Jessica have been at the forefront of numerous local and national high profile grassroots campaigns for racial and social justice including the black supplementary schools movement of the 1960s and 70s, the Black Parents Movement which protested against the controversial 'Sus' laws and mobilised organised legal representation for Black and Asian people arrested during the Southall riots of 1979, the New Cross Massacre Action Committee. Bogle L'Ouverture Publications Limited has published pioneering books by Walter Rodney and Bernard Coard.

In June 2014, Doing Nothing is Not an Option, a biography by Margaret Andrews, was published by Krik Krak, and launched at the Victoria & Albert Museum.

Thanks to the Crowdfunding Campaign by Huntley Family members and Friends on 13th October 2018, there was an unveiling of the Eric and Eric Huntley by the Nubian Jak Community Trust at the Huntley's home in Ealing, also the 5th anniversary of the passing of Jessica Huntley. The Nubian Jak Memorial Plaque is a timely recognition of the contributions made by Jessica and Eric Huntley to Black British experience for more than 50 years.

Sally Baffour *Patron*
Ghanaian-born, Sally Baffour, came as a student to the UK in the 1970's. A former interior architect, after adopting twins she found herself advocating for appropriate rights and services for them. She was soon head-hunted to sit on Adoption Panels for Children's Services for several Local Authorities in London and became a Trustee of the British Association for Adoption and Fostering (BAAF). She has advised extensively on Black perspectives, therapeutic and parenting needs of children in care and set up several self-help forums for carers.

Sally set up the Thank U non-profit organization, which in the UK runs the Discussions Across Generations programme for young graduates and Youth Relief Talent showcase that motivates disenfranchised young people to contribute to the welfare of others by building on their talents. Thank U has forged links with Community work in Africa and the Caribbean. Supporting grassroots Charities for children and the elderly.

Its main focus is on building Community libraries in rural areas and is currently establishing three major libraries in honour of the iconic world-renowned author, the late Maya Angelou, in South Africa, Ghana, and Trinidad & Tobago.

Amongst its awards Thank U has received the 2006 -Won 'The Heart of the Children's' Award for the Best Charity, from the Third Dimension Gospel Reggae Support Organisation.

Manjinder Chijarh *Proof Reader*
Manjinder Chijarh graduated at Kingston University (2010) in Creative Writing with English Literature (BA Hon). Joining WAPPY in 2014, initially as a volunteer Drama Workshop Assistant, he soon wrote an article about WAPPY for the Ealing-based, free quarterly, Neighbours' Paper, which he has also been volunteering for. From 2017 Manj joined the board of trustees and accepted an invitation to be one of the anthology's co-editors. He has also been volunteering as an 'Event Coordinator' with Poetic Word, since 2018. It's a community organisation working to promote the Arts in Hounslow, West London. In his spare time, Manj creates insightful prose and thoughtful poetry that has inspired students and artists alike. In addition, he enjoys graphic novels and self-help books, regularly tinkers with software and helps out at charity events.

Alydia R. Thompson *Artist*
Alydia R. Thompson is a London-based Fine Artist who graduated from Middlesex University in 2016. She is a passionate multi-medium based artist, heavily influenced by representations of her cultural past, be it through examples of art, dance or music. A Black-British artist of Jamaican heritage, Alydia's artwork documents her interpretations of the diasporic Caribbean culture in British society in many forms, as she aims to inform educate and inspire others. She has exhibited in several collective exhibitions including, Incite Insight In Site, Islington Arts Factory 27/2 - 5/3/2015 Black Nation, Events Week 2015, The Atrium @ The Grove Middlesex University Watch this Space (for one night only), Beaconsfield, Vauxhall 16/3/2016 The Wider Art & Design Degree Show and Old Truman Brewery 06/2016.

Lindsay Warner *Proof Reader*

Award-winning writer, Lindsay Warner, is currently studying for a degree in English Literature at the University of Exeter, set to graduate in 2019. Her debut published poem in 'Middlesex Poets', at age 10, was one of the main inspirations behind WAPPY's birth. She started participating in its workshops and events from the summer vacations of 2009, since this May, has been volunteering for the organisation by helping to deliver the recent Near Neighbours funded Building Bridges workshops, and is also one of the editors of this anthology. As part of the London Metropolitan Archives' 2018 Spring Festival, Lindsay was interviewed by five WAPPY members about her writing process and journey from WAPPY to university.

WAPPY AUTHORS

1. Laith Abed (2018)
2. Maisa Abed (2012-2015)
3. Sara Abed (2012-2018)
4. Adeola Aderibigbe (2016-2018)
5. Sarai Aidoo-Richardson (2017-2018)
6. Daniel Alawode (2011)
7. Mohamed Ali (2017)
8. Mariam Allawi (2014)
9. Malak Allawi (2012)
10. Yasmin Allawi (2012)
11. Isiah Ansah (2017)
12. Shania Bajaj (2018)
13. Julia Baramo (2012)
14. Sami Baramo (2012)
15. Keegan Bloom (2012)
16. Emma Boundy (2012-2014)
17. Leika Boundy (2011-2014)
18. Jessica Bruley (2012)
19. Shelay Busby (2012-2013)
20. Darcy Carter (2013-2014)
21. Tamzin Chapman (2013-2017)
22. Shanice Coleman (2008)
23. Charlotte Corcoran (2009-2011)
24. Teagan Courtney (2018)
25. Renée Dawkins (2013-2018)
26. Marianne Deutsch-Bruce (2014)
27. Leila Drummey (2018)
28. Leilani Drummey (2011-2018)
29. Zion Duncan (2009-2013)
30. Jai Ellis (2009-2014)
31. Ben Eshun (2010-2015)
32. Christian Ferguson-Dawkins (2015-2018)
33. Emelia Ferreira (2012)

34. Lillian Ferreira (2012-14)
35. Yasmine Fetit (2013-2014)
36. Niyil Gayle-Jackson (2008)
37. Nazir Gentry (2014-2015)
38. Isla Heath (2014)
39. Luke Heinlein (2011-2015)
40. Maddy Heinlein (2011)
41. Jessica Howard (2015-2018)
42. Maia Hicks (2013-2014)
43. Pierre Ikong (2018)
44. Athena Ioannou (2017-2018)
45. Christopher Ioannou (2015-2018)
46. Tehannalee James-Palmer-Skeete (2018)
47. T-Khai James-Palmer-Wahome-Kellehey (2017-2018)
48. Jack Joshua (2015)
49. Lola Joshua (2015)
50. Cassius Jackson-Callen (2010-2015)
51. Georgiana Jackson-Callen (2008-2015)
52. Gerda Kleinberga (2014-2017)
53. Daniel Larbi (2011-2012)
54. David Larbi (2009-2013)
55. Michael Larbi (2009-2018)
56. Paul Larbi (2011-2012)
57. Sarah Larbi (2018)
58. Louis Leeson (2017)
59. Jessica M Howard (2015-2018)
60. Majd Mansour (2012)
61. Acquaye McCalman (2008-2018)
62. Mary Mikhaeil (2012)
63. Miriam Mikhaeil (2012)
64. Aaliyah Momoh (2017-2018)
65. Anaya Murrell (2018)
66. Ida Mwangi (2012-2015)
67. Mark Mwangi (2012-2017)
68. Amin Nabizada (2014)

69. Marwah Nabizada (2014)
70. Kyra Nelson (2012-2018)
71. Rana Omar (2014)
72. Reem Omar (2012-2014)
73. Ivy Oppong (2014-2018)
74. Santanna Otalvora-James-Palmer (2018)
75. Izoje Owaka (2012-2015)
76. Zephaniah Pascal (2014)
77. Henrietta Perry (2009-2013)
78. Effie Quansah-George (2010-2018)
79. Ashley Robert Wadsworth (2018)
80. Kieran Ross (2011-2018)
81. Honey Ryder (2014)
82. Balin Shah (2009-2013)
83. Jasmine Shah (2010-2011)
84. Kaiaanu Shepnekhi-Boston (2012-2015)
85. Mesentis Shepnekhi-Boston (2012-2015)
86. Kai Sim (2011-2018)
87. Seren Sim (2011-2018)
88. Grace Simons (2011-2012)
89. Finlay Sokal (2018)
90. Talia Sokal (2018)
91. Maisha Thomas (2014)
92. Shangwe Thomas (2013-2014)
93. Aniyah Thompson (2016-2017)
94. Dewaine Thompson (2016-2017)
95. Kai-ern Thompson (2015-2018)
96. Kiki Thompson (2016-2018)
97. Centelia Tuitt-Walker (2017)
98. Chad Turney (2015)
99. Imara Turney (2015)
100. Sonam Ubhi (2010-2012)
101. Riley Vaughan (2017-2018)
102. Sasha Vaughan (2017-2018)
103. Shahidah Victor-Sampson (2011)

104.   Nyah Walcott-Quansah (2014-2018)
105.   Quincey Walcott-Quansah (2018)
106.   Lindsay Warner (2009-2018)
107.   Nathan Warner (2008-2013)
108.   Savannah Wight (2013)
109.   Ricari Wilson (2017)
110.   Tristan Wisdom (2018)
111.   Robyn Wisdom (2018)

WAPPY ILLUSTRATORS

Maisa Abed
Sara Abed
Walid Alqaddah
Leilani Drummey
Athena Ioannou
Acquaye McCalman
Ivy Oppong
Effie Quansah-George
Kai Sim
Fransica Simmonds
Alydia R Thompson